THIS SIDE
OF BREATHING

By: Jenni Waldron

For all those desperate to experience
life on this side of breathing.

I'm desperate, too.

TABLE OF CONTENTS:

ACKNOWLEDGMENTS

I have been far too blessed in this life. Not that life has been easy, or painless, but it has been made rich.

By my God whose name I am altogether unworthy to write about, let alone worship – except you insisted to redeem me from my deepest darkness to give me new life and purpose. May you be blessed by these words and all my words.

By my family who stubbornly refuses to give up – the big family and the small one. To my husband, Richard, you are the greatest man I have ever known. Thank you for leading me to the heart of Jesus, both in the beginning and every day since. To my kids, Ryder and Jayne, thank you for being so uniquely yourselves. If you plan to keep on growing up, I will have to keep on growing, too.

By my community who insists on loving well. My definition of family has grown to include a deep and wide spread of broken people committed to becoming like Jesus together. To my friends who call me out of my brokenness and to the feet of Jesus, may you never stop. To my church who is so committed to share the story of our God, may you be bold and brave.

It is still strange to me to have written a book, but I am so grateful for the opportunity to share the freedom I have found in a life led by the Spirit. Thank you, Mark, for challenging me to write. Thank you Karen, Crystal, Dad, Jessica, Steve, Kara, Kevin, Jen, Eleisha, Wes and Josh for your time editing, contributing and encouraging me along this process.

Now for the fun part . . .

AN INTRODUCTION

Have you ever felt out of breath – as if you have been trying everything you can think of to breathe – and yet you are still stuck, breathless?

Maybe you've been running hard and you're out of breath because the sheer amount of energy you have been pouring out has cost you almost everything.

Or you've been holding your breath, waiting for the worst to come, or pass . . . afraid to open your lungs to receive what is waiting for you.

Perhaps you've been sick. You've tried everything to clear a path for the oxygen you are craving, but still – the difficulty remains.

It could be the shock. You've had the wind knocked out of you. Something you did not expect and could not have prepared for has collided with your life, and now you find yourself trying – and failing – to breathe.

The first time I remember getting the wind knocked out of me I was 8 years old, and I wanted desperately to be a gymnast. My friends and I would play "Olympics" and do tricks together during recess at the private school I attended in

Texas. In our school uniforms, we would perform our tumbling feats and even embark on a few group routines.

During one such afternoon, I was chosen to be the top of a pyramid. One of the girls was less-than-steady, and she just so happened to be positioned on the bottom of the pyramid. Physics would say this was going to turn out bad for me. Only seconds after I climbed to my place, down I dropped from the height of 3 elementary-aged girls standing on top of one another – directly onto my face.

It felt like minutes before I could breathe again – minutes which felt like eternity.

Something that had always been natural, so automatic as breathing had become a seemingly impossible task in that moment.

My chest heaved and my body ached. I was both desperate and aware of my desperation. It frightened me.

Breathlessness is terrifying. This is true in our physical lives, and it's true in our spirits.

Just like we experience moments of exhaustion and sickness and shock in our physical life, our spirits face problems, emotions, and circumstances we can't seem to get around, let alone through.

I assume you are holding this book because you or someone you love has had the breath knocked out of their spirit. You know you are not well, or the pace at which you are living your life is exhausting. You just want to breathe. We all just want to breathe.

It is in those moments, like our bodies strain for breath, that our spirits strain for God.
"Where are you in this?"
"Why can't I hear you?"
"Where did you go?"
"Where can I find you?"

We think, *"If only I could pray the right prayer or make the right choice, I would be able to find God. I would be able to experience Him. I would be able to get through this."*

What if God isn't something to be chased or conjured or found, but someone to be received?

What if it's just like receiving breath?

When God spoke us into existence, He didn't stop at words – the God of Creation breathed into dust and life was formed. In that moment, man was filled with the very Spirit of God. Life was given as a gift, through breath.

Every baby has a first breath. It's a pivotal moment when a child begins to breathe.

Our spiritual lives are no different. When a person

learns to breathe in the Spirit of God, it changes everything.

Jesus said in John 3:5-6 (NLT), *"I assure you, no one can enter the Kingdom of God without being born of water and the Spirit. Humans can reproduce only human life, but the Holy Spirit gives birth to spiritual life."*

The Holy Spirit is a gift of life – a gift many of us complicate, but it is a gift we have already been given. The most natural thing our spirits can do is to breathe in the Spirit of God.

It is my hope that through the words on these pages you will learn how to receive the Holy Spirit, and through your learning, you will see there is nothing you could face that you cannot breathe through.

Together, we will learn to breathe in the Holy Spirit through:
Problems we cannot see a way around.
Emotions that scare us and keep us stuck.
Circumstances which seem to be hopeless.

What would it look like for a community of people to live truly full lives?

What if our kids were to grow up in homes full of peace and not fear?

What if we could learn to process our emotions instead of becoming slaves to them?

What if we believed that life was never meant to be lived in isolation?

Might we see with new eyes that anxiety and fear and hopelessness have no hope to stand against the power of the Holy Spirit in each of us?

Would we see that even death cannot take our breath away, when that breath belongs to the Spirit of God and is given as a gift?

Would we finally believe that nothing is too dead for our God to bring back to life?

That, my friends, is my deepest prayer and most fervent desire.

Through your openness to His voice and by His power, which raised Christ from the dead, may the Holy Spirit lead you into a fuller and deeper life than you could imagine for yourself on your most creative day.

A POEM

I need Him like I need oxygen and slow, deep breaths.

I need Him like I need the signals between my brain and lungs to remind me to breathe, even when I am in a deep sleep.

I need Him, desperately, in the moments I've been holding my breath, striving to reach the surface, and my whole body hurts from the lack of Him supplying my soul with Himself.

I need Him to push out the pollution I let in as He pushes in, life-giver, leading me to one more moment in which I need Him.

My need for Him is my gift from Him.

I need Him like I need oxygen and small moments reminding me to breathe. Yes, you are running . . . out of breath, but you can still breathe – in through your nose, out through your mouth. It takes focus and intention and calm. I need the calm. I need Jesus in the running and in the resting and in the racing and in the calm.

I need Him like I need to raise my arms, opening my lungs – I need to raise my arms and say – I am out of breath. Me. Right here. And it hurts. I need more of You in this moment.

I've been running fast and I forgot to breathe and now . . . You can revive me. I need You to revive me.

Me, with my anxious soul – my tired soul – my wandering and lost soul – my empty soul – my mourning soul – my breathless soul . . . me . . . right here in this moment.

And in the moments I forget to need You.

I need You like I need oxygen and slow, deep breaths.

I'm breathing now

Slow, deep breaths.

Slow.

Deep breaths.

A STORY

---

like I need oxygen.

OXYGEN

My husband Richard and I, were sitting in a counselor's office, facing one of the hardest things we could imagine. We were holding hands – *at least our marriage is safe*. We were so scared. It felt like we were losing everything. *So, this is what tragedy feels like – it's no one's fault, but that somehow makes it worse. If I can't blame anyone, how can I get past this?*

Have you ever faced something too big for you?

It hurt. It was confusing. Life felt so very close to unraveling. The more I thought about it, the worse it got. As if the thoughts themselves were fuel to the fire threatening to destroy us. Time was spinning, confused between freezing and speeding up. I was lost within the past and the future at once. And the present – too painful. I couldn't be in the present. That would have to wait.

He, the counselor, spoke, drawing me back to the couch in the office – with the tiny window – not enough light. *"Why is there so little light? Don't you think a good counselor's office would be well lit? I bet I could help them with their ambiance. Yes, I'll help them. I'll tell them there should be more light and bigger windows – and maybe less paperwork."*

He said two things that day: "I can't help this get better, but I can teach you how to breathe through it."

"He can't help . . .
He can teach me to breathe?"

Breathe through it? I couldn't breathe. He was right. I couldn't breathe, and I was stuck on one side of my problem with no bridge to the other – just a chasm of 'what ifs' and 'can't we justs' and 'it's not fairs' where the way forward should be, once was.

One side. The other side. *"How do I get from where I am to where I know, deep in my bones, I am supposed to be?"*

I stood looking at the edge of the cliff where a bridge should be, where I remember once seeing one, and was frozen by the effort required to rebuild.

There is so much to do, to prepare to rebuild. So much stone to clean up and haul out. *"I don't know if I can handle that right now."*

All to get to a clean slate, *"I am desperate for a clean slate."* The rubble could be cleared and the plan could be made, but still, the rebuilding. All this effort expended only to end up with a bridgeless place – no way to the other side – maybe less wreckage, but still no bridge.

"Is that the best I can hope for? Less damage, but no resolution?"

I couldn't breathe. That's what the counselor said. Well, he said I COULD breathe, but I would have to learn. I would have to open up my lungs to receive.

I would have to receive slowly, he said. In through my nose. Breathe slowly so as to not overwhelm my lungs – I was so very overwhelmed. Slowly:

> Start at the bottom. Picture the air entering your toes. Draw it upward toward your shins, don't think about your lungs just yet. Slowly, draw the breath to your knees, then your hips. Slowly. You control the speed of it. You control the depth of it. Slowly up through your stomach to your lungs, but it doesn't stop there – your chest rises and your face receives the breath as you picture the oxygen reaching the very tip of your hair.

Don't rush to release it. This is life in your bones. Slowly on the releasing, too. Slowly. This time out of your mouth, pursed lips. Slowly, like a song. Your body sings of the nourishment and control. Control. I no longer feel so overwhelmed. I can choose how much oxygen I need. I can choose to receive it and to release it.

In the quiet, this truth rose above all the shouting of my fear and uncertainty: everything may be out of control, but I can breathe.

And in the time that I am breathing, life is moving. Moments are passing and progress is progressing. I am breathing through it.

You may be at a bridgeless place. This place may be new – or it may be a lost place. But all the lost things can be found. All the broken things can be healed. All the dead things can experience life.

You can learn to breathe through it.

LIKE A DIVE

On vacation in Cancun, they taught us how to scuba dive in the 5-foot-deep pool at the resort. It was a beautiful day and my class clown of a husband, Richard, kept making me laugh while under the water. That was really inconvenient because it made my face scrunch up and water pour in through my mask – the opposite of what you want to have happen when you are under water breathing through a tube.

We learned how to correct laughing moments (pressure on the forehead, blow out through your nose to clear the mask), and how to allow your ears to pop to relieve pressure.

There is always the eventuality that your mouthpiece will fall out, and you don't want that. Luckily, there is a handy button that blows the water out to prep it to flow oxygen again.

We need that oxygen. The oxygen tanks are heavy on land, but so important. Air is everything when you are 30 feet below the surface – plus the water lightens the load.

Flippers. Mask. Tank. Waiver – should you die or be seriously injured . . . *"yes, this is a fun afternoon activity."* I looked around. No lawyer huts were to be found on the beach to update our will *("Give the coin jar to Ryder, don't spend it all in one place, son; Jayne, my princess of a daughter, can have my fake pearls")*, so I guessed it couldn't be too dangerous.

Out on the boat and into the water we went. Everyone in our group jumped in, and we all took turns slowly lowering ourselves, managing the pressure deeper into the water.

I didn't expect everything to change so drastically beneath the surface. Under the water, in the pressure, everything feels different.

I hadn't really thought about how LOUD the world is until I was under it, in the pressure. In the water, the noise fades away, broken by the weight and mass around me.

It's eerie to know that even if I cried out, in addition to having a mouth full of water, no one would hear me.

My feet hit the bottom of the ocean . . . okay, not the actual bottom of the ocean . . . we were only graded for 30-foot dives. But, still . . . I could see the expanse of the water above and all around me. I now know what Ariel in The Little Mermaid felt like when she looked up to see the broken sun rays deflected in every direction casting light on the surface – the surface at which I could breathe.

Everything was slower, darker, calmer, stranger.

Vision was limited.

I got a little lost once. Richard came to find me. Then we got a little lost together. The reef was so beautiful, but the panic of losing sight of our instructor made the pressure and quiet and dark more ominous than it was before.

We found him. Scratch that – he found us. Turns out there are always wanderers on dives – seems right we were the wanderers.

Isn't that the Gospel? He found us: wandering,

confused, distracted by what we think is beautiful or worth it.

Jesus came into the depths of our world, facing the same pressure we face, and He led us through it – into a new life marked with breath and fullness. We are all wanderers, but we are not alone. Even the bottom of the ocean has a voice which commands it, a Creator who knows its depths and lengths and immense pressures.

Even on the bottom of the ocean, though my voice is caught and cannot carry, the God who made the ocean sees me. The God who made me hears me. And He is carefully, patiently, leading me through the pressure and the depth.

With the direction and sight of the instructor, we traveled through our dive and safely returned to the surface to shake out our ears and breathe.

The clarity of that day hit me weeks later.
I had experienced anxiety before in my life, but I never had a way to describe the feeling until I went scuba diving.

It's like all the weight of the world caves in around me. I'm on the bottom of the ocean with sight lines to the surface, but no breath and no sound and no speed. The sheer effort needed to get to the surface keeps me stuck like concrete in the space where I reside inside my anxiety.

Have you felt like that? Like the pressure and the depth are at odds – the depth of your feelings at war with the pressure to stop feeling them?

Pressure shapes space. Pressure shapes us.

New baby. New house. Job loss. Diagnosis. Epiphany. Conflict. Mistake. Big mistake.

Pressure.

It's a gift, pressure. Most of us spend our whole lives trying to avoid the pressure that is needed for us to grow. Ultimately, we spend our whole lives avoiding growth.

That is not for us. The life we have been called to is a deep life. The life you have been called to is a deep life.

So, our lives are like a dive – learning to manage the pressure and the depth. The more you descend into the deep parts of life – the greater the pressure. The greater the pressure – the more you have to focus on breathing.

Remember the oxygen. It's in the tank. It might be more complicated on the ocean floor. You have to focus. Don't scrunch or rush. Screaming won't help – just breathe. In and out. Intentionally. In and out. The breathing moves the pressure around you.
The breathing displaces the pressure and makes a way for forward progress.

The breathing fills our anxious souls with the oxygen we desperately need, the oxygen we were made to receive upon our creation by our Creator.

We have an unlimited supply of life from the Life-Giver, should we choose to breathe.

At the foundation of the Earth, before man set foot on this planet, God intended and designed that He would give himself to us – in every way.

As Father – to love us unconditionally.
As Son – to be the sacrifice for us, to redeem our brokenness.
As Spirit – to sustain, to comfort and to fill us with breath and life, over and over again.

Maybe you haven't heard this yet, and maybe you just need to be reminded of the deepest truth to combat the pressure and depth of the confusion of our messy lives: You, with your anxious soul – your tired soul – your wandering and lost soul – your empty soul – your mourning soul – your broken soul . . . you . . . right where you are in this moment . . .

The Holy Spirit is oxygen for your breathless soul.

And you can learn to breathe.

---

deep breaths.

RIDICULOUS

Have you ever been reading something, and all of a sudden you realize the word you just read was totally wrong? Your mind either skipped over something or replaced a word with one that made no sense in context.

It's like those Facebook posts that declare you are a genius because your brain can decipher a word with only the first and last letters in place, while all the others are scrambled. *[SIDE NOTE: I love being told I'm a genius.]*

So, the other day as I was reading something, my mind did this exact magic. It's a verse I've read a million times – it's on my fridge right now, actually. With my brain in secret and full preparation to punk me, I read, *"Let the message about Christ, in all its*

ridiculousness *fill your lives* (Colossians 3:16, NLT)." I noticed in maybe a split second the word exchange my brain made. The actual verse says *in all its richness* . . . but, to be honest, my first thought after this switch was . . . *"Well, it is kind of ridiculous, isn't it?"*

To believe that the least among us will be the greatest. To follow the example of a man-who-was-God who allowed himself to be innocently murdered. A man who took everything I believe is natural in relationship and turned it upside down to say that the greatest form of love is self-sacrifice. A man who forgave before forgiveness was sought. A man who kissed those who betrayed him.

Our Jesus, who taught that being great does not matter when compared to being redeemed . . .

It is utterly preposterous that God would enter the ugly, broken world we live in and submit Himself to pain, that He would not set Himself up above His people in a place of safety and authority, but would choose the life of a servant . . . a blue collar worker . . . a radical.

It actually confuses me at times, in an *"I'm super mad"* kind of way, that when God became human and came into our world, He did not come to overthrow corrupt governments or to free the slaves trapped in untold evils . . . at least not in the sense I understand freedom. I get angry that He didn't fix the problems that seem to be the most

urgent around me.
He didn't fix my problem.
My problem is really big, Jesus. I need a bridge.
I could really use your help . . .

How upside-down and utterly fantastic is it that God actually believed that what needs the most reform is the human heart?

The symptoms are not the sickness. Is it possible that our problems are not as pressing as we may believe?

The greatest need in our world is for the Spirit of the Living God to fill us, to fuel us, to lead us.

And, how ridiculous of Jesus to believe He could make that available to us.

I think He knew. I think He knew the depth of need in me, and that only He could show me that need.

When I see Jesus, I see how arbitrarily my own efforts will end. I see that all of my life is only a brushstroke in the masterpiece of the whole story of creation and redemption and newness. I see that even my most pure intentions are like mopping up water without stopping the spill.

Only a ridiculous message of self-sacrificing, heart-altering, redemptive, non-expectant, before-the-foundations-of-the-Earth kind of love could

22

actually change anything – maybe even EVERYTHING.

Jesus knew that the only way for us to learn to live, to breathe, would be for us to watch Him do it.

This is the way: we realize our need and see that our victory over the battle we are facing is nothing in comparison to the glory Christ has set before us.

Maybe our story is bigger – more ridiculous, more rich – than we think.

BREATH

378 times. That's how many times the word *ruwach* shows up in the Old Testament. Some of those times the Hebrew word is translated breath.

> *. . . as long as my breath is in me, and the spirit of God is in my nostrils . . . Job 27:3 (ESV)*

> *They went into the ark with Noah, two and two of all flesh in which there was the breath of life. Genesis 7:15 (ESV)*

> *By the word of the LORD the heavens were made, and by the breath of his mouth all their host. Psalm 33:6 (ESV)*

> *How can my lord's servant talk with my lord? For now no strength remains in me, and no breath is left in me . . . Daniel 10:17 (ESV)*

Biblical Hebrew words are more complicated than English words. Well actually, they are simpler. They have no vowels – it's the translation that is complicated. Bible translators depend heavily on context and contemporary writings to determine the right translation of a single word. Many times, there are varied translations for the same word. Take *ruwach* – breath, right? Well, more than 200 times, translators write the word 'Spirit' when they read that word:

> *The earth was without form and void, and darkness was over the face of the deep. And the Spirit of God was hovering over the face of the waters. Genesis 1:2 (ESV)*

> *. . . And he has filled him with the Spirit of God, with skill, with intelligence, with knowledge, and with all craftsmanship . . . Exodus 35:31 (ESV)*

> *Then the Spirit of the LORD was upon Jephthah . . . Judges 11:29 (ESV)*

> *And the Spirit of the LORD began to stir him . . . Judges 13:25 (ESV)*

Think about it this way: I say, "I love brownies."

That's a normal statement – and very, very true.

I also say "I love my family." Please tell me those mean different things. And, maybe a language other than English would use 2 words to differentiate, though we only have the one in English . . . See the point?

Context. Culture.

There is another Hebrew word commonly translated as breath: *nĕshamah*. Want to know how that word is also defined in that culture?

You got it – SPIRIT.

It seems like even more closely related than my love of brownies and my family is this relationship between the words BREATH and SPIRIT. Is it possible the translators of the Old Testament knew something we do not, or in the very least, something we have forgotten? That our very breath is so deeply tied to our Spirit it is almost indistinguishable.

SPIRIT
Then God said, "Let there be light," and there was light. Genesis 1:3 (NLT)

"Then God said . . ." this theme would repeat itself throughout the creation account. Genesis, chapter 1 repeats over and over again that God SPOKE LIFE into existence. Space, time, plants, animals . . . and then, the rhythm changes. It's like when music takes a turn.

We are all jiving together on a driving beat, and all of a sudden the kick drum drops out and the keyboard sustains an airy pad – or the rhythmic and calming finger picking pattern on the guitar shifts to a strong strum, or the band drops out all together and just the voices sing a song of unity with rising harmony and bold melody . . . a shift – intentional and beautiful.

God spoke life into existence – and then God said, *"Let us make human beings in our image, to be like us. Genesis 1:26 (NLT)*

God said let's make people . . . but how did He do it? Shift.

We'll have to look further, to Genesis 2:7 (NLT) . . . *Then the Lord God formed the man from the dust of the ground. He breathed the breath of life into the man's nostrils, and the man became a living person.*

God spoke. Day and night ruled the earth. God breathed and man became a living person. Shift. Not just speaking – this time, breathing. Not just existing – this time, living.

Have we missed something vital? When God breathed life into man, He put His Spirit into him.

Only into people did God breathe His Breath. Without the breath of God, we would be dust, or at best, bones and flesh. It is not a mistake that God chose to breathe into people to give us life.

God set forth a foundational rhythm in that

moment – that Life and Spirit mark His most prized creation.

Can we really separate our spirit from our physical life? Many of us try to . . .

But, like Daniel cries out, *"There is no ruwach left in me"* . . . no breath . . . no spirit – when we are empty and tired and alone and drained, we are lacking spirit. We are lacking life.

God's Spirit interacting with our God-given spirit leads us to Life.

When we breathe in physical air, we keep the oxygen and release the carbon dioxide. It's science and it's a story . . . Creation Art meant to direct us to the Life-Giver. Receiving the good – traveling to every corner of our body, deep into our spirit – and pushing out the bad meant to suffocate us, physically and spiritually.

To receive oxygen is to receive life. To expel carbon dioxide is to defeat death.

To receive the Holy Spirit into our busy, anxious, confusing lives is the only true way we could ever find life, but there is pollution here within us, sin that so easily entangles. The Breath of Life can push it out as we receive the Spirit of God.

Darkness extinguished by Light.
Pride pushed back by Humility.
Doubt proven weak by Faith.

Death overcome by Life.

It gets even better. I saved the best part for . . . well not last . . . but right now.

The Old Testament is translated from the original language of Hebrew. The New Testament was written in Greek.

Breath isn't as popular a word in the New Testament as it was in the Old, but the word does appear – three to four times depending on your translation. There is a word *pnoē* that shows up once. Every other time the word BREATH is mentioned, it's translated from the word *pneuma* – which just happens to be the word most often translated as . . . wait for it . . .

The Holy Spirit.

In fact, of the 385 times *pneuma* shows up in the New Testament, 226 times, Holy Spirit or Spirit of God is what we read in our language. (The others are varying forms of spirit, just without 'of God' attached.)

I don't think it is a coincidence that as Jesus shows up on the scene – our perfect picture of Life embracing and receiving the Holy Spirit – the word for breath is almost forgotten in favor of spirit. Jesus has always been the great dot connector. It's almost as if when face to face with Jesus, we can finally understand who the Holy Spirit is. We are introduced to the power of God and our ability to receive it at once.

When Jesus died, resurrected and ascended to heaven, He sent His Spirit to be our comforter, to be our Source, up close.

In fact, after Jesus rose from the dead, He appeared to His disciples and did something remarkable.

He came to a locked house, showed Himself to the disciples *(see the holes in my hands? My side?)* and then . . . *he breathed on them and said, "Receive the Holy Spirit." John 20:22 (NIV)*

Wait.

Jesus, the Son, who was present at Creation, who was raised to life by the Breath – the Spirit – of God just did something incredible.

He shifted the rhythm. 100 percent access to the Holy Spirit. In this moment lies the clearest picture of the divine connection between Breath and Spirit laid out in scripture. It is that natural. It is that sacred.

Breath created life – Breath resurrected life – Breath imparts the Spirit of God. There is always more. As many times as you can inhale, God can fill you. He never runs out.

The Creator God not only breathed into us at

creation, but now breathes into us each time we open the lungs of our souls to receive Him.

Do you see it?

The Holy Spirit is oxygen for your soul. He is the breath that will give you LIFE.
No other source can sustain you but the Breath who created you.

So, how can we receive the Spirit of God?

I'll suggest three stops on a journey to receiving:

1. Admit that you are not enough.

We face life unfulfilled, uncertain, and unable to measure up to all the pressures we will face. At the end of the day, your energy is gone, you have to rest. There is a beginning and an end to you.

There is wisdom in accepting your limits. Our striving to be enough is only a distraction from all the goodness God wants to pour out onto us when we are ready to receive Him.

This not enough-ness is not a secret. We know we don't measure up. In fact, our failure is often what keeps us from God. Hear this clearly: our failure may keep us from God, but there is nothing able to keep God from us.

We are so focused on our inability to reach some

arbitrary threshold of "enough" that we miss Jesus, who offered Himself to be enough for us. God is not surprised by our falling short. In fact, He went to great lengths to ensure our failures would not have the last word in our stories. Jesus ensured with His sacrifice that our failure would always shrink back in defeat when faced with the overwhelming love of the cross and the undeniable power of the empty tomb.

One of my favorite authors, Jennie Allen, said in her book *Nothing to Prove*, "To get to the place where God can be enough, we have to first admit we aren't."

We have limits. God is limitless. We have a beginning and an end. There is no end to God. We fail. God forgives.

We are nowhere near enough. God has never asked us to be enough. That is a role He fulfills better than any of us ever could.

2. Recognize His power.

Have you ever tried to give a little kid medicine?

I have two kids: a boy, Ryder and a girl, Jayne. They are red-heads, and they work hard to live up in every way to the reputation of every red-head who has gone before them. I call them the little gingers. Stubborn and opinionated, they know exactly what they want and how they want it. Rarely is medicine the thing they want.

But, ice cream? This story is epically different. From fits thrown for hours just to force one teaspoon of meds down their sweet little throats to desperate pleas for more ice cream – just a little more, please!

Jayne, the littler ginger, was really sick once, the kind of sick that just breaks your heart. She wanted to feel better so badly, she was actually compliant with our requests to rest and take her medicine. She got to the point that she begged for more of the nasty liquid because she knew it was her salvation – the only thing that could lead her out of the way she was feeling in that moment. She recognized the power of the medicine in her life.

Our openness to receive the Spirit of God is directly related to how we perceive the power of the Spirit of God.

Could this Spirit really give me new life? Can Jesus really change everything for me? When you believe that the same power that raised Christ from the dead breathed life into Creation – you begin to see that the dead things in you can be raised – you begin to trust that you can breathe and things will change.

3. Receive the Spirit of God in the way He first gave it to us.

'Then the Lord God formed the man from the dust of the ground. He breathed the breath of life into the man's nostrils, and the man became a living person.'

We allow God to create and re-create in us – by breathing in the Breath He gives. By stopping and waiting and slowly receiving that which was always intended to sustain us.

Imagine in this moment your soul has lungs – open space ready to receive all that God wants to fill you with. Systems ready to expel anything that would be pollution to your Spirit.

God put in us a rhythm of receiving and expelling.

Breathe in.

Breathe out.

Breathe in.

Breathe out.

Be filled. Allow God to purify your spirit. Slowly now.

Picture it starting in your toes.

It's at your knees now.

Up through your hips.

Don't stop at your lungs.

Draw the breath up through your shoulders –
picture it flooding your face – to the very tips of
your hair.

Slowly on the releasing, too. Pursed lips.

Slowly like a song.
Let the reminder of the ability to receive flood over
you as you release your breath, trusting there is
always more.

There is always more.

---

small moments reminding me to breathe.

HOME
I walked in the door – tumbled is more accurate. I couldn't really walk.

The kids were at a friend's house for the next couple days so my husband and I could process.

Process was the last thing I wanted to do.

Rage. Yell. Cry. Run. Defend. Defeat. Be understood. Be released. *"Yes. Any of those."*

I sat on the ground in a puddle of my own tears running through all the things which would make this better – all of them centered around myself.

In each scenario played out in my mind, the battle

had to be short – or I didn't know if I could survive.

I don't believe our God works the same way in short battles as in the long ones. Oh, yes, He works, but there is something about the length of a thing that adds significance.

A 60-year marriage, a life-long friendship, a 40-day fast in the wilderness . . .

The length of the thing was my biggest fear. *"How long can I withstand this? How long can I survive? How long can I do this . . ."* Me. I.

I was stuck right smack dab in the middle of my problem, drowning in my own self-focus.

I think a lot of times we get stuck looking at ourselves and caring only for ourselves because it is even more painful to look outside of our own circle of tears to the circles of others.

Outside our circle lies the heartbreak of those we love, the unfulfilled dreams of the generation before us – and further still – the poverty of relationship those around us face – not to mention the true poverty most of the world lives in every day. And slavery. The slavery is there too. Real, actual slavery. Undeserved and seemingly unabated. And what about the people stuck in the slavery of their sin who don't know there is another way, a breath of life who can sustain them in a way they never imagined.

"I can't do this right now. My problem is too deep, too close. I can't look outside my circle of tears on the floor by my fireplace."

Sitting there on the carpet, I heard a voice – one I could not ignore.

I heard these words: Remember the Truth.

I had been believing the lies. I had forgotten they were lies – that I'm not enough, strong enough, that I should run, defend, give up, give in . . . and who was I hoping to defeat?

"I am not alone. I do not live in spiritual poverty without substance or source. I am not stuck inside this circle."

The Spirit inside me began to lead me to a gentle, but firm re-set of my perspective.

I got out the 3x5 cards from my bag I was saving for some project at work. While I listened to words that fed my soul sung from my Spotify account – on repeat – I began to write.

One verse. Then another. One truth, followed by many, many more truths.

As I filled each card with a truth from scripture, my spirit began to take slow, deep breaths.

It started in my toes and began filling my whole body with the Breath of Life – I was learning to breathe.

I don't know how long I sat there receiving, writing, believing, remembering. But, when I was done, I had enough cards to line the walls of my entire house, so that's what I did.

I filled my home with a solid thread of truth. This was a battle – and it would be long, so my strategy had to be good, and there is only one proven battle strategy when your enemy is a lie: to seek and believe the truth. To defeat a lie, you must live as if the truth is the strongest weapon in existence, because it is.

One by one, I took a piece of double-sided tape and posted a truth on my wall. Side by side, the truths stood at eye-level, everywhere I looked. There was a physical Belt of Truth around my home.

This project took hours. Or days. I don't remember. I do remember this: I was breathing through it. This was not the end.

Every time I walked the walls of my house, I was filled with the same Spirit who raised Christ from the dead – I can face my battles. I can face my sadness and my disappointment. I can face my anxiety and fear. I don't have to have a resolution or know the end of the story when I know the process is still progressing . . . when I am breathing through it.

At my fingertips, at any time, is the Spirit of God – all I have to do is inhale.

DEEP BREATHING
Good, deep breathing is one of the best ways to combat overwhelming emotions. This is a physical practice that completely alters your body's response to stress. According to the American Institute of Stress, deep breathing leads you into something called the relaxation response:
- Your metabolism decreases
- Your heart beats slower and your muscles relax
- Your breathing becomes slower
- Your blood pressure decreases
- Your levels of nitric oxide are increased

How we long to feel this way! Not anxious. Not afraid. Rested.

Our souls carry the same craving.

Writing down scripture and posting it around my house is more than a story, it's a strategy, a technique – a holy practice.

2 Timothy 3:16 (NIV) says this: *All Scripture is God-breathed and is useful for teaching, rebuking, correcting and training in righteousness . . .*

All Scripture is God-breathed.

I looked up the word in the Greek – the core thought is this: Scripture is inspired by God.

This is a deep thought, and deep thoughts take some digging. So, go with me here:

The word "inspire" in English has 2 main meanings *(According to dictionary.com)*:
1. fill (someone) with the urge or ability to do or feel something, especially to do something creative.
2. breathe in (air); inhale.

To fill. To breathe.

The words on the pages of scripture were filled the same way we were filled – with the Breath of God.

Did you catch that? The power that fills you and me when we receive the Spirit of God – the resurrection power – the same power that raised Christ from the dead – is poured out onto the words we read every time we open the scriptures.

So, reading, meditating on, remembering, trusting the words of scripture is a literal breathing in of the Spirit of God.

I have a friend and mentor who starts every day with 5 deep breaths – of scripture.

Slowly, breathe in – spend time reading, chewing on, digesting the words. Breathe out your gratefulness to your God who is close and active.

And again.
Breath in – truth. Breathe out – gratefulness.

5 deep breaths every morning.

It will put your spirit into the relaxation response.

TIME TO BREATHE

Sometimes you can read something or hear something, and you just need some time to process it. At a few points through this journey of learning to breathe, we will take a time-out.

It's your time to stop and think – to breathe.

In each "Time to Breath" section, I'll suggest a practice in experiencing the Holy Spirit in your own life through whatever you are currently facing. Feel free to try what I suggest or spend time in your own way connecting with God and listening to His Spirit.

I bet you can guess the first practice:

TRUTH CARDS
What you'll need:
- 3x5 cards (or pieces of paper you already have lying around)
- Sharpie – *I just like Sharpies – sharpies make things feel more important.*
- Bible *(or maybe your phone with the Bible App or biblegateway.com)*

What you'll do:
Do you have a favorite verse? Start there. Write down on the first card the truth of scripture that comes to mind. Then, the next one. Maybe look

through your Bible to the verses you have highlighted or underlined. You'll see that God has already been speaking to you – you've been learning to breathe already.

Don't have a favorite, yet? Is scripture unfamiliar to you? Websites like BibleGateway.com and the Bible App are easy to search for a specific word. Some Bibles even have topical indexes you can reference to speak to whatever problem you feel like you are facing. Maybe start with "grace" or "forgiveness" and see what speaks life to your soul.

Once you've written until your spirit feels full, post the scripture in places you will see it. When you read and meditate on the words of scripture, you will find you are breathing through whatever it is you are facing, and in the process, you will be getting to know the nature of God over and over again.

I can't resist listing a few of my favorite starting points on the next couple pages:

*Yet I am confident I will see the Lord's goodness while I am here in
the land of the living. Wait patiently for the Lord. Be brave and
courageous. Yes, wait patiently for the Lord.*
Psalm 27:13-14 (NLT)

*The Lord is my light and my salvation— so why should I be afraid?
The Lord is my fortress, protecting me from danger, so why should I
tremble?*
Psalm 27:1 (NLT)

*Don't worry about anything; instead, pray about everything. Tell
God what you need, and thank him for all he has done. Then you
will experience God's peace, which exceeds anything we can
understand. His peace will guard your hearts and minds as you live
in Christ Jesus.*
Philippians 4:6-7 (NLT)

*I look up to the mountains— does my help come from there? My
help comes from the Lord, who made heaven and earth!*
Psalm 121:1 (NLT)

*Your unfailing love, O Lord, is as vast as the heavens; your
faithfulness reaches beyond the clouds.*
Psalm 36:5 (NLT)

He has removed our sins as far from us as the east is from the west.
Psalm 103:12 (NLT)

*So be strong and courageous! Do not be afraid and do not panic
before them. For the Lord your God will personally go ahead of you.
He will neither fail you nor abandon you.*
Deuteronomy 31:6 (NLT)

*For we are God's masterpiece. He has created us anew in Christ
Jesus, so we can do the good things he planned for us long ago.*
Ephesians 2:10 (NLT)

And may you have the power to understand, as all God's people should, how wide, how long, how high, and how deep his love is.
Ephesians 3:18 (NLT)

And since we are his children, we are his heirs. In fact, together with Christ we are heirs of God's glory. But if we are to share his glory, we must also share his suffering. Yet what we suffer now is nothing compared to the glory he will reveal to us later.
Romans 8:17-18 (NLT)

Now all glory to God, who is able, through his mighty power at work within us, to accomplish infinitely more than we might ask or think.
Ephesians 3:20 (NLT)

This means that anyone who belongs to Christ has become a new person. The old life is gone; a new life has begun!
2 Corinthians 5:17 (NLT)

And God will generously provide all you need. Then you will always have everything you need and plenty left over to share with others. 2 Corinthians 9:8 (NLT)

And I am convinced that nothing can ever separate us from God's love. Neither death nor life, neither angels nor demons, neither our fears for today nor our worries about tomorrow—not even the powers of hell can separate us from God's love. No power in the sky above or in the earth below—indeed, nothing in all creation will ever be able to separate us from the love of God that is revealed in Christ Jesus our Lord.
Romans 8:38-39 (NLT)

So let's not get tired of doing what is good. At just the right time we will reap a harvest of blessing if we don't give up.
Galatians 6:9 (NLT)

PROBLEMS

desperately.

Have you heard this: the safest way to be in a car crash is to be asleep? It's because your body is relaxed, not tightening in ways which could cause you injury.

What if we faced our lives rested and relaxed of spirit? When the crashes come – and they will come – we may face less hurt and quicker healing.

We can't predict what problems we will face. I don't think many of us would raise our hands to say our life has turned out exactly how we dreamed it would, and those who would are lying to themselves.

Negative experiences in our lives do not necessarily equal a negative outcome. Don't get me wrong, you may not see the problem in your life pan out to be the beautiful story you have written in your mind,

49

but there will still be beauty. The God who made you has promised that.

And we know that all things work together for good to those who love God, to those who are the called according to His purpose. Romans 8:28 (NKJV)

That's how I have that verse memorized. Have you heard that scripture before? It's often quoted to me when life gets messy.

> *"Oh, Jenni, remember, God works all things for good."*

> *"Yes, this is so terrible, but God works all things for YOUR good"*

> *"Jenni, remember that God is working for YOUR GOOD."*

PAUSE. Full stop.

Is it possible that when God said all things, He meant it? He meant that He is working on a grander scale than we can imagine? That His purpose for us could be to allow pain and suffering and loss to shape our character to become more like Him?

When I read that verse, I inserted my name into it: for the good of Jenni.

When did I become so arrogant? (Obvious answer is always, but really?)

How could I possibly believe when the God who made the entire universe says the words "all things" that He would be directly referring to all things pertaining to me?

What if all things in your life is this: To become a person of such deep and empathetic character that the children you raise become world changers for the Kingdom?

Or, what if all things is something you never get to see? If our God works outside of time and human limits, then His impact is not bound by either.

We are stuck in our timeline of birth-to-life-to-death.

God created that timeline.

Do you see that our *perspective* is broken? And if our *perspective* is broken, then our *assessment* is broken.

We stand on our cliff, staring at our problem and the chasm to get from where we are to what we see as the other side, and God is on a completely different cliff!

Our problem is deeper than we know.

We have a vision problem.

Vision is the interpretation of light around and

through objects, and that task takes up 30 percent of our brain!

It takes a lot to interpret light in our mind, and light is constantly changing.

Light is one of the most powerful forces in our physical world. I love photography. Photographers have to interpret light constantly. Morning light is different than evening light. Light appears in different color hues at different angles at different times.

Have you ever gone on a road trip and found yourself in the middle of nowhere in the middle of the night? I am often surprised by how much light there is in the night. I can remember nights living in Montana in which I was driving and didn't even need my headlights because the light was so vivid.

Day, night, morning, evening. Light changes so much, or does it?

I've never been to outer space, but I will assure you I have seen lots of movies about space. I also lived in Houston when I was a kid, so I basically run NASA.

There is something strange I have noticed when observing space: the sun is always bright.

There is not night and day and morning and evening for the sun. Because our day and night are based on the Earth's relationship to the sun.

The sun just shines, and the moon looks quite dark. It is lit by the sun in space, but it doesn't "glow" the way we see it from earth.

The way we see it. It's all about perspective.

Light seems to change because of what stands in between us and the source of light. Clouds come. The Earth shifts and turns. Our vantage point changes tirelessly.

It's what stands in between that makes it seem like light changes.

It is our problems that block our vision. Our problems confuse us and lead us to believe we are hopeless from our vantage point.

In my life, things often change without my permission and out of my control. Life just goes. Sometimes I feel on top of it, and other times I am left grasping for a hold of 'What . . . just . . . happened?'

In those moments, I feel like I can't see God in the midst of my problem.

I have found comfort in realizing that the light itself is not dependent on my vantage point or timeline.

Even in darkness, the light wins. When I realize

that all I have to do is look beyond what gets in between, I can see God even in the most hopeless situation.

Perspective is everything because vision is limited by vantage point. We need to see things from God's perspective to believe there is hope in hopelessness. To do that, we have to slow down, take our eyes off our problem and focus on Jesus.

We must allow our spirits to relax, trusting that "all things" is so much bigger than us – which must mean our God is so much bigger than we have made him.

We can rest in His provision. We can rest as our Spirits are filled with more and more of Him.

We can relax and release control, because it never belonged to us anyway. Our problems, though they are real and vast, lose their power over us in the perspective of God.

So how do we learn to see in a new way? What will change when we do?

REBIRTH
I have a friend who planned a water birth for her third pregnancy. It made me so curious. How can the baby breathe?

Throughout a pregnancy, oxygen travels to the baby through the umbilical cord in all the extra blood mom pumps out. Babies' lungs start working at around 10 weeks, but only to practice and build the muscles. They are sort of pointless biology at this phase, just for practice.

I read that at birth, temperature change is actually what prompts a baby to breathe. In a water birth, the water is set to the approximate temperature of the inside of the momma's body. When the baby is born into the water, the temperature stays the same, so any water the baby takes in, she swallows. She is getting all the oxygen she needs from the cord.

When the baby meets the cooler air, she opens her lungs and breathes. Once she breathes, only oxygen through her lungs will do to sustain her life.

The cord still provides oxygen for a little while, but once her tiny lungs have a taste of life, she is now dependent on it.

That's it!

We are all made in the image of God. Our very humanity is marked with the likeness of God and access to His Spirit. Like infants who haven't yet taken a breath, many of us spend our whole lives thinking this is everything – pointless biology, just practice. Practice for what?

What if life was meant to be more? What if these lungs inside our souls, when we learn to use them, actually lead us to the most FULL LIFE. Once we taste true, full life, nothing else will do.

No other source can sustain us but the Breath who created us.

What if we don't have to spend our lives searching to find God? What if He has already marked us with the ability to connect to Him? What if our very lungs are proof that God has placed all we need to belong to Him inside of us?

Is it possible that this is why Jesus told Nicodemus in John, Chapter 3, that we have to be born again? We have to open our lungs and breathe. We must cut the cord to the life of simple and separate humanity – humanity apart from God, and step into a new life – a life in which receiving the Spirit of God is as innate, and vital, as breathing in and out. *Ruwach*.

I understand I am simplifying the concept of the Holy Spirit.
I am intending to.

Our God is an artful foreshadower.

It is no coincidence that a baby is born with every bit of biology he will need to grow, eat, love, heal, become a father, and breathe. We were created from the very beginning with everything we need to belong to God.

A baby can go nowhere, become no one, without

learning to breathe.

I have a friend who is a neo-natal nurse. She treats the tiny babies – the ones who come to meet us too soon.

She told me the mark of sustainable life is the ability to breathe on one's own. Babies can be born in terrifyingly early stages of their momma's pregnancy and make it. Why? Because their lungs can be used. With the very little ones, there are machines which can help the baby's lungs to function, but the lungs have to be developed for the machines to work.

I had lunch with a respiratory therapist who took this further for me. The most specific difference between a baby who makes it in the early days and one who doesn't is both the function of the lungs and the body's ability to manage the pressure equally throughout the body. New babies, even the full term ones, are at risk for Patent Ductus Arteriosus, or PDA. Essentially, they could have an abnormal blood flow which will result in unequal pressure. Maybe you've seen the nurses come in to take the blood pressure of a baby's left hand and right foot? They are checking to see if the baby is handling the pressure effectively.

The ability to sustain equal pressure once blood is flowing and being filled with oxygen is the real mark of sustainable life.

Yes, you can inhale, but can you get that oxygen to all the places it needs to get to? Is there a blockage, a closed off artery? Is there a reason why your left side can receive oxygen, but the right is struggling?

Oxygen + Pressure is what keeps our physical bodies alive. Could it be the same with our spirits? We need the pressure to live. The problems we face are met with the oxygen of the Holy Spirit flowing to each area of our lives as we learn to trust God more.

It's when the pressure gets inconsistent – one problem starts to stand out more than others – that help is needed. We have to find and remove the blockage.

We have to see what is keeping that area of our life from experiencing God.

The mark of a sustainable spiritual life is the ability to breathe, to receive the Holy Spirit, and to see His love, wisdom and peace permeate our entire lives.

SUSTAINABLE & GROWING

It always bothered me in my earlier days of following Jesus when people would refer to me as a "baby Christian." I just wanted to be taken seriously in my faith. I felt this way until I watched my son throw a fit about wanting to be a BIG BOY when he was 2. He was so angry he couldn't "do it myself." I realized then what it is like to be a believer who is growing in maturity. I desperately wanted to become a mature believer. I wanted to experience the wisdom and understanding, but I wanted to skip the growing part. We all have a 2-year-old inside of us who desperately wants to skip the steps of spiritual growth to get from where we are to where we know we were designed to be.

I want my son to grow to be a man who loves and follows Jesus, who trusts the voice of the Holy Spirit, who loves his wife and kids well, who works hard and gives without expectation. To become that man, he will have to experience ups and downs in this life. He will need to learn to work hard first in school. He will need to love his sister well to learn to love someone else. To become, he will have to walk the road of becoming, and it isn't a race.

God wants us to live our deepest calling. It was, in fact, He who called us. And since it was He who called us, we must go to Him to develop us.

Like our kids depend on us to feed them, help them rest, give them medicine, offer them comfort, our God has given us the same opportunity to depend on Him.

Jesus said, "And I will ask the Father, and he will give you another Advocate, who will never leave you. He is the Holy Spirit, who leads into all truth." John 14:16 (NLT)

We learn to receive the Holy Spirit the way we first received Him, by breathing in the gift of life He offers freely. After the receiving, there is still the developing. There is a cultivation of the spirit which leads to a rich and growing spiritual life.

Picture your soul like a garden. A garden can be planned and planted perfectly, but left uncultivated, it will not thrive – and ultimately, not live.

How do you know if a garden is thriving?
By its yields.

I have a friend who is a gifted gardener, and her home is always full of fresh basil, lettuce, mint and even peppers and squash.

Real talk: I planted peppers once. I was sure I would be able to grow them. I had the right amount of sun and good soil. I had the seeds and put them in the ground just like my friend instructed me to do. Then . . . nothing. No fruit. No yield. Guys, I can't even grow strawberries – and berries are essentially weeds.

There is one reason my gardens fail: I never water them. Oh, I intend to water them, but . . . life.

Maybe you learned to breathe and have experienced God in your life, but feel stagnant. Maybe you have some parts of your life, the resilient parts, that are still growing while some are left abandoned, uncultivated.

God desires that we become all He has designed us

to be. He wants to see all of us fulfilled, growing, vibrant and thriving.

We know if we are growing by the yield.

Scripture gives us a beautiful metaphor of the signs of spiritual growth.

In the letter Paul writes to the people in the region of Galatia, he writes: *But the Holy Spirit produces this kind of fruit in our lives: love, joy, peace, patience, kindness, goodness, faithfulness, gentleness, and self-control.* — *Galatians 5:22-23a (NLT)*

If you grew up in the church, this is a familiar passage to you. I remember this being quoted to me when I was being impatient, unkind, or any of the antonyms of this sweet fruit.

I was told to learn to cultivate the fruit of the Spirit. I tried harder and harder and still ended up making choices that looked a lot more like me than like Jesus.

Here is the best part about this picture, so don't miss this: You are not the gardener. You are the garden.

The fruit of the Holy Spirit is not the fruit of your efforts, but of your submission to become more like the person of Christ.

You can't become kinder. You have all the kindness

you contain already – but the Spirit can fill you with His kindness. You can't become more patient, but the Spirit can fill you with His patience. It's His fruit, not yours. But you get to be the garden that bears the fruit.

That fruit is the evidence that you have watched how Jesus lived and are allowing His Spirit to lead you to become more like Him.

It is the yield of the Spirit in you, given to you to enjoy as a gift that builds a sustainable spiritual life.

It is in the nature of fruit to yield in season – and fruit, like apples, need other fruit to yield a robust and full harvest.

Our spiritual life is a progression, a journey, a garden. It is not a road easily walked alone.

You will experience seasons, which you cannot control – you might experience harsh winters, hot summers, fruitful autumns. You will see fruit again, if you allow your Spirit to be cultivated.

How do you know if the fruit you are seeing really is the fruit of the Spirit?

In testing.

The easiest way to know if you have grown in the Spirit is by watching how your spirit reacts to problems, emotions and circumstances you don't understand and cannot control.

My natural response points all the arrows back to me. As I submit to the work of the Holy Spirit in my life, I'm able to see from God's perspective – and, if I'm patient enough, maybe even experience things far beyond what I can do on my own.

The best part about our God is He loves to give good gifts.

Life in the Spirit is full, truly abundant. You will find strength you never knew existed. You will gain knowledge you did not have before. You will be led to do incredible things outside of your comfort zone. You will experience and take part in wonders only God could be responsible for (see: the entire book of Acts). Most important, you will see the family of God grow and thrive as you help those around you learn to breathe in the incredible gift of the Holy Spirit.

**in through your nose,
out through your mouth.**

IN THROUGH YOUR NOSE
Inhale. Breathe in.

This is step one. And it's a hard one.

Breathing is not physically hard, at least not for
most of us. My brother had really severe asthma as
a kid. Most of my young memories include him
sitting in Dad's recliner with a breathing treatment
over his face, watching us.

I always wanted a REAL Christmas tree. We lived
in southeast Texas when I was a kid, so a nice
evergreen was not something you go and cut down,
and my parents always said no to a real tree. I

always wanted my Christmas to look like the movies – snow and tree cutting and scarves and beanies – then I took 4th grade geography. What a sad thing it is to grow up.

My brother was allergic to everything. Really, all the trees and pollens and flowers. So, nothing that lived OUTSIDE could come INSIDE. Allergies are the worst, so was his asthma. My brother spent almost every winter hooked up to the breathing treatment 6 times a day, until he had surgery that opened up his respiratory path in a new way.

My husband and I and our 2 kids live in the Pacific Northwest. I love the PNW. It's beautiful and surprising, and sunny days are like a special shipment of gold that everyone cashes in on together with long hikes and late night campfires.

And, there are evergreens here.
It is the evergreen state . . .

Our first married Christmas, I begged my husband to take me to cut down a tree. He didn't understand why it was such a big deal since his family had always cut down their Christmas tree – he had lived here his whole life.

Ultimately, because he is a smart man, I found myself out in the middle of the woods on a small tree farm smelling delicious pine and the hot cocoa available for sale at the hut to my left.

I breathed in deep. And then I sneezed.

Nope. Not gonna let this get me down – we will have a real tree in our house for Christmas this year. It went on that way for 3-4 more years. Jenni insists on a tree. Richard obliges. Jenni is miserable in the house for the whole season battling *(ignoring)* her allergies. It was a happy life.

Finally, the dream wore off, and we got a fake tree. Can I tell you – I really hated sweeping up pine needles. My life is so much better now.

Allergies are one of my least favorite things. I just want to BREATHE!

In through my nose–ACHOO–dangit.

Did you know that allergies are the result of an oversensitive immune system? Basically, we experience allergies when our bodies over-react to something which is actually harmless.

I think I may have an allergy to being tickled. Something harmless, which makes you over-react. *Oh, sorry I just kicked you in the nose, babe . . . but you were tickling me . . .*

Now that I think about it, I'm starting to think I may be allergic to lack of control. I know for certain I have an allergy to problems I face.

I over-react, do you?

Yes, our problems can cause us pain, hurt and general discomfort – but the problem doesn't have to derail us. I am much more bothered by the symptom of my allergies (runny nose, itchy eyes, coughing, wheezing, etc.) than the cause of my allergies.

For example: I really like dogs. If I pet a dog and then touch my face, I will be miserable for a day. Dog – fine. Allergies – not fine.

I know what I'm allergic to, and I know how to treat it. Could we recognize the way our spirits react to problems we face and learn to breathe through them?

Could we realize the problem isn't the enemy, but rather our over-reaction?

Our bodies fight off infection using histamines. When we experience an allergic reaction, the histamines are released in large cell groups (called mast cells) to fight the potential threat in our bodies alongside the antibodies in our system. The problem is that too much misdirected histamine can be dangerous, sometimes even fatal (epi-pen anyone?).

We have to get the enemy of our spirit right, or else we will misdirect the histamines of our spirit to fight things which are not worth fighting and end up in more pain than when we started.

The problem is big and scary and real. But the problem is not what is causing you not to breathe; it's your refusal to inhale. Or it may be your anxiety leading you to hyperventilate leaving you with shallow breaths and not enough oxygen to sustain your life.

How can you breathe deeply, even when you are afraid?

Most doctors I've spoken with have said breathing through your nose is the most effective for a good, deep breath. It's not physical as much as it is psychological. It's easier to manage a slow breath when you breath in through your nose.

You aren't overwhelming yourself with too much, too fast. You can likely get just as much air, but your ability to calm yourself could be lost in the process. Can we be content to slow down when we are facing difficulty? Can we take slow breaths as to not hyperventilate our spirits? Manage the intake. Slowly.

Everyone is different. Some people have asthma, some have allergies and some just get to cruise through life on the easy train. But we all at some point have to make a conscious effort. It's the same with your soul.

Get the help you need to get and make the changes necessary to get good, clean oxygen into your soul. For my soul, inhaling looks a lot like sitting in the quiet and writing. What is it for you? What reminds you of the goodness of God? What brings your perspective into check so you see things more clearly around you?

Did you know your eyes need oxygen? Of course, your whole body needs oxygen, but our sight is heavily affected when we can't breathe well. It's hard to make good, healthy choices on where to go and what to do when you can't see clearly.

Everything depends on this.

What fills you up?

When God created us, He put a rhythm into our physical bodies – inhale, exhale. While we are allowing our souls to be created and re-created, we need this rhythm, too.

I believe deeply in "finding your place." That's not a reference to discovering who you are or what career you should have.

Find your place to be with God.

Jesus did this. You'll notice throughout the gospels Jesus went away to find a place. He would go into the mountains to olive groves and gardens. I sometimes wonder if He loved gardens so much because they reminded Him of the First Garden. The beauty of creation as it was always intended to be. Full of harmony – clean air – pure relationship.

Jesus would go away to be with the Father.

At every home we live in, I like to find "a place." Once it was my giant, ugly, old blue chair in the corner of my bedroom. Once it was an upstairs deck. In one house, it was the front porch. I liked to sit on my yoga mat (on which I most definitely did NOT practice yoga).

I faced west. I tried facing south and east, but for some reason, west was right.

Someone recently asked me how I find space to hear the voice of God in my life. How quickly the answer came to me surprised me. I don't find space as much as I find a place.

I love to wake up early in the morning and go outside when it's cold – sweatshirt, winter socks and hot coffee kind of cold – and watch the morning come. I really like contrast. Being warm while cold surrounds. Cold reminds me of God. Not that I think God is cold . . . but because I can still find warmth in the cold. You can always add more layers and more blankets to make you feel warm in cold. God is always able to add warmth in any circumstance. I deeply believe there is no situation too dead for God to bring back to life.

Do you have a place? If you don't, find one. When we put ourselves in a posture to receive, the receiving comes more easily.

70

You know this – when you need to take a deep breath, you straighten your posture, lift your head. Can we submit to allow the Holy Spirit to do this with our souls?

Straighten our direction. Lift our heads and our hearts to the perspective of heaven, and let heaven pour into all the deep and hidden places in us.

And, when we've been sitting here a while and our hearts are full of Spirit, we release the breath, out – beyond us.

OUT THROUGH YOUR MOUTH
The cry.

You know the moment . . .

I'm guessing you have experienced the birth of a child – either your own, or on a movie.

First comes the waiting, the expecting, the breathing, the pushing.

Then, the silence.

When our son was born, I thought that silence would last forever. It was the most painful, terrifying moment I had yet to experience.

Breathe, son. Breathe.

It's not so much that his lungs didn't have air

already in them, but could he release it?

Can we release it? Can we let go of the things we hold on to? Good and bad? Can we trust that the Life-Giver will meet us in the exhale with a fresh bit of oxygen. We do not live in a poverty of Spirit. We live in an abundance. Can we release and make more room for the Goodness and Grace and Spirit God has waiting for us.

In that hospital room, the seconds passed like hours – every breath was held hostage within anxious lungs, until . . . that sweet, piercing cry was released from the tiniest of lungs, leading us all to exhale, too.

Relief released into the room as we held the proof that this little one would be able to breathe.

From our very first breath, we learn to receive and to cry out. The danger of breathing is we don't only inhale oxygen, as our world is imperfect.

There are other gases there. So, we have to learn to exhale.

According to the National Heart, Lung and Blood Institute, what pushes our subconscious bodies to breathe is actually the level of carbon dioxide in our blood. Your body has sensors which read the levels and send signals to your brain to remind you to breathe when there is too much pollution in your system.

Without clean oxygen for just 4 minutes, we risk brain damage or even death.

There are two main types of illness which make it difficult to breathe: obstructive and restrictive.

Restrictive disease makes it difficult to inhale – think pneumonia restricting space in your lungs because of the fluid building; or pulmonary fibrosis, which scars the lungs causing the passageways to thicken, making it hard for air to get to the right places.

Obstructive disease affects the ability to exhale. When my brother was facing his asthma battle, he could get air in, but could not get the air out effectively. You've heard someone wheezing? My respiratory therapist friend told me the wheezing is a good sign. Of course, the best would be clean and free breathing, but wheezing at least shows some air is getting out.

I wonder if some of us have an obstructive disease in our spirits. Are we hanging on to things we should be releasing? Is it making us sick? Slowing us down? Can we let go?
We have to discover our ability to release the pollution, whether it is past mistakes, inability to forgive, fear, control, selfishness . . .

When we breathe out through our mouths, we give the biggest opening to expel the pollution within us.

There is something to that, isn't there?

Breathe in through your nose – be careful of what you allow into your spirit. Be generous with what goes out.

Many of us have this dangerous tendency: we hold on to things that can destroy us. Maybe we chose to inhale them, and maybe they just came in with the rest – but the pollution has got to go.

As a teenager I experimented with the party lifestyle. I remember the first time someone handed me something I was supposed to inhale. I took a puff and my lungs revolted. Lots of coughing, my eyes watered. My lungs were created to protect my body from harm. It got easier with time, which is not a good thing. Now, years later, my lungs have healed with the lack of pollution. They have remembered what clean air feels like, tastes like, and I crave it.

Remember, we are called to a Deep Life – nothing but the best for the lungs of our souls. Why do we make it harder than it has to be for ourselves?

The more sin we allow in and the longer we allow sin to live within our hearts, the more confused we become about true Life. Our souls adjust to sin, and that is a tragedy. When we allow our souls to comfortably co-exist with sin . . .

Contentedness is confused with Entitlement

Satisfaction is confused with Addiction
Strength is confused with Rebellion
Love is confused with Insecurity
Healthy relationships are
confused with Unforgiveness
Joy is confused with mere Happiness

Sin steals our Life away. *The enemy comes only to steal,
kill and destroy . . . (John 10:10 NIV)*

If the enemy can distract you from the Life-Giver
long enough –

you're too busy
you're more important than that
you are so misunderstood
you can have anything you want

you . . . you . . . you . . .

– then the next best thing becomes the necessary
thing. And the necessary thing becomes the only
thing. Soon enough you forget what it means to be
truly alive.

It's like living in smog and thinking the air is clear.
It might be clearer than yesterday or down the road
or in so-and-so's town, but it is not clear.

Do not confuse the real thing for the counterfeit.
Don't let pollution choke out your soul and
become familiar.

Just like your body was designed to identify the carbon dioxide and expel it, your spirit was built to hear the voice of the Holy Spirit and follow Him into all truth.

How do you expel the pollution of sin?
You have to release it.

There is a word I have avoided most of my life of faith. The word is confession. It felt so formal. Confession.

Maybe this confession thing is not as scary as I've made it out to be.

Let me outline for you a few of the common conversations in my life:

Jayne: "Mom! Ryder hit me!"
Me: "Ryder, say sorry."

Ryder: "Mom! Jayne broke my toy!"
Me: "Jayne, say sorry."

Me: "Husband, you hurt my feelings . . . Say sorry."

Friend: "I've been feeling hurt and left out."
Me: "Sorry."

Say sorry. These two words may have been among the first words of correction I shared with my kids. There are tons of blogs about whether or not to have your children use this phrase, but I just ignored them all, because, well, people should say sorry.

It's just a fact of life. We hurt each other. When we hurt each other, amends feels necessary.

It's as if each of us has a jar full of scraps of paper with good feelings written on them. When someone hurts you, they take some of the good feelings out of the jar. At this point, there are two options. Leave the jar lacking what it once held, or refill the jar with amends and more good feelings.

I'm someone who likes to hear the words, "I'm sorry." I like to hear them, and I'm quick to say them.

I just want people to have full 'feelings jars'. I'm not good at letting broken situations sit idle, without progress. If I say sorry sooner, then the feelings can be replaced in the jar sooner, right?

This would make perfect sense if relationships really were like an inanimate jar full of scraps of paper – and oh, how I wish they were.

We know this, don't we? A relationship isn't a math problem. 1+1 does not always equal 2. The goal of my relationships cannot be to get through life with individual jars full of good feelings, but to become a community of people who share all of life together.

The goal of relationship is not individual happiness

– but collective intimacy.

In my friendships I want to understand and meet real needs, not just enjoy each other's company.

In my family, I want us to know each other deeply and share unselfishly.

In my marriage, I want 1+1 to equal 1. Oneness as the goal, not just teamwork.

I can get on board with this in my physical life pretty easily, but what about with God?

I fail all the time. I let sin in. I don't take time to expel the pollution from the lungs of my soul. I know who I am supposed to be, and how I'm supposed to follow Jesus, and I miss it.

It feels so much scarier to "say sorry" to God than to people in my life. It's not like God has a jar of good feelings He needs me to fill, but there is the whole "I died for you so you could have a full life" thing . . .

I think confessing my sin is so hard because I'm afraid to come face-to-face with my guilt, my shame. I already know I fail all the time, so taking extra time and heart space to talk about my failure with God feels like cruel and unusual punishment.

Here is an important and encouraging truth: confession leads to intimacy.

I want intimacy with God.

You cannot have intimacy without honesty. It's one thing to know something about someone you love. It's another to know that they are aware of it, too. So, we confess – to each other, to God.

Imagine what it's like for God, who knows everything. The patience and grace He has with us as we learn to accept our failure is astounding.

When I fear confession, I am really saying that I don't believe God's grace is big enough for my sin. I believe that if I share where I fall short I will have to deal with the brokenness in me, and I don't have a cure. Refusal to bring my sin before Jesus is really just a refusal to believe He is who He says He is.

Confession is not about shame. It's about grace.

The enemy may have come to steal, kill and destroy, but your Jesus says to you today, *"I have come that they may have life, and have it to the full." John 10:10 (NIV)*

Full life. All of you. Jesus isn't just after the good parts, He's after intimacy.

What kind of marriage would I have if I told my husband I only wanted to take part in the good parts of him? Refusing to work through the hard parts? We are two imperfect people learning to love one another. It's messy, and it's beautiful.

The best part about relationship with Jesus is there is only one imperfect person in the mix, rather than two. The potential for beauty is even higher.

I am imperfect. Jesus is perfect – and He is perfectly willing to help make me more and more like Himself, by the work of the Holy Spirit within me.

The enemy wants to steal the full life Jesus wants to give you by keeping you slave to the sin inside your heart.

When we allow the Holy Spirit to point out the sin entangling us we are free to exhale, releasing the brokenness. We are trusting that the sacrifice of Jesus is more than enough to fill in the gaps of our stories. Confession leads to intimacy, and intimacy leads to repentance.

Repentance is a 180-degree turn from the place you have been. This is what heart change looks like.

Confidence that Jesus fills in the gaps and the Holy Spirit can lead us to full life is what a life marked with repentance looks like. This is true with God and with those we love. Once you offer up your confession that you have not measured up, you will be met with true grace – and you'll never want to go back to that place of sin and pain again.

It's not so much that you won't fail, but you will fail within the sweet embrace of Jesus.

That's the place I want to stay – within the sweet embrace of Jesus where there is always more grace.

You do not have to settle for the next best thing – you don't have to live almost full. Only the most full life for you who are loved by God. Oneness. Fullness. Freedom.

ACCESSORY MUSCLES

Sometimes, our pollution sensors get broken. We can't see it anymore. We can't feel the difference between life and death – between wisdom and sin – and we are dangerously confused as to which one will lead us into life.

In biology, there are muscles referred to as accessory muscles. Accessory muscles are muscles not normally utilized for breathing. They are on your neck and chest and step in when the regular respiration becomes labored or inefficient.

Who are your accessory muscles? Are they active? Are they engaged in your life?

Who can step in to help you breathe when your faith begins to fail? Who can help you recognize the sin threatening to suffocate your spirit? Who are the people in your life who will be sensors for your soul?

Find actual people you can rely on and ask for help. None of us walk through life unscathed or without challenge. The difference between those who give up and those who don't comes down to who you are walking with.

When the people of Israel were making their way through the wilderness they came up against many obstacles. One such obstacle were the Amalekites. Moses was leading his people into a new, free life – but thing after thing kept coming in their way. Hunger. Thirst. Armies. Desert.

What do you do when you face obstacles to your freedom?

Moses led the people to fight. Joshua took some men out to lead the charge against the Amalekites, and Moses held up the staff God had given to him. When his hands were up, the Israelites were winning the fight – when he dropped his hands, they began to lose.

Look at what scripture says happened when Moses got tired and couldn't hold up his staff any longer, *"Aaron and Hur found a stone for him to sit on. Then they stood on each side of Moses, holding up his hands. So his hands held steady until sunset." Exodus 17:12 (NLT)*

They saw that he was tired and couldn't keep going, so Aaron and Hur held up Moses' arms.

Accessory muscles.

They held him up. We need each other. None of us can do this alone.

The people you choose have to know what you are going after. What is your goal? Moses had people to protect and an army to defeat. He was well aware of the battle he was fighting.

If your goal is to please the Lord and be a part of healing this world, and your friends see you wavering – that's when they step in to lift your arms and to help you breathe.

Plainly, you are no use to the mission of God if you are not alive.

Find friends who will lift your hands because they believe in you and, more importantly, they believe deeply in the healing name of Jesus and the power of the Holy Spirit to work through us.

This is a battle that can be – and will be won. It's a long battle, but all the good ones are.

TIME TO BREATHE

Let's take a moment to pause. It's time to breathe.
I've suggested 2 practices below.

ACCESSORY MUSCLES
What you'll need:
- Paper/Journal
- Your calendar
- Some time

What you'll do:
Who are your people? Not just the ones who you
like to see at parties. Write down the names. There
probably won't be a lot of names on your list. Many
of us will have 2-5 names of people who can truly
help us breathe.

1. Write down the names of people who you
   rely on spiritually.
2. Set up a coffee date, walk or dinner
   conversation with at least one of your
   people.
3. During that time, ask each other this
   question: How is your soul? If your soul was
   a balloon, would it be inflated or deflated?
   Share how you can support each other.

YOUR PLACE

What you'll need:
- Paper/Journal
- Pen
- Some time
- Some courage

What you'll do:
Whatever your place may be, schedule 30 minutes alone there as soon as you can. It may help to put on some worship music. Spend some time journaling or writing down, in your own way. the things you know you need to let go of. Let's start with the big stuff. Is there anything standing in the way of you receiving God fully? Is there sin you are holding on to you need to release?

Once you have identified the things you know you need to exhale make a point to share your process with one of your accessory muscles. Let them know you are letting go, so they can celebrate with you as you experience more and more life.

EMOTIONS

---

even when I am in a deep sleep.

SLEEP

Am I the only one who gets a little weirded out by our bodies' ability to function without conscious control? It's like the Internet, which I can't even BEGIN to understand . . . space stuff . . . satellites . . . rooms with wires. My head hurts.

My husband is the deepest sleeper I have ever met. It's terrifying – and terribly annoying.

Let me explain a normal morning in the Waldron house (on a morning I plan to sleep in):

5a –   My alarm goes off – I reset for 6:30a
         #beautysleep
5:45a – Richard's first alarm goes off. Richard does
         not hear alarm. I press snooze.
5.52a – Richard's second alarm goes off. Richard

does not hear alarm. I press snooze.

5:54a – Richard's FIRST snooze alarm goes off. He hits it.

5:58a – Richard's third alarm goes off. He hits it.

6:01a – Richard's FIRST snooze alarm goes off, again . . . He hits it.

6:03a – Richard's SECOND snooze alarm goes off. He hits it.

6:07a – Richard's THIRD snooze alarm goes off. He hits it.

6:10a – Richard's FIRST snooze alarm goes off, again . . . this is getting ridiculous

6:12a

6:15a – This is a new alarm . . .

6:16a

6:19a

Everything in me wishes this was an exaggeration. The man needs 12 or more alarms to wake up in the morning from the depths of his sleeping mind. Yet he is still alive every morning. His body was not too asleep to remember to breathe. He was able to continue to inhale and exhale all night long.

Have you ever felt like you were sleeping through your life?

Like everything keeps moving around you, but you aren't on the same train?

ALARMS

Are you a snooze button person? I'd categorize myself as an alarm re-setter. I'll set my alarm a little early and reset it to trick myself into thinking I'm "gifting" myself with more sleep. Sometimes I'll press snooze a time or two.

I think we do this with our emotions.

Emotions are not a bad thing – God created emotion. At their deepest core emotions have a very significant purpose in our lives.

Emotions are the alarm clock for our soul, intended to alert us to something we need to check in to.

You are standing on the edge of a very high cliff – Fear kicks in – BEEP BEEP BEEP – so you become aware of your proximity to bodily harm.

Someone you love passes away – sadness – alarm – to alert you to your need to process your loss.

Your kid says "Dada" for the first time – joy – alarm – don't miss this, this is the good stuff.

Emotions are meant to wake us up. To remind us that there is more to our lives than what resides within us. There is a whole world out there to interact with, to impact, and to receive.

Some of us go through our lives hitting our emotional snooze button – *"I'll feel that later"* – *"I'll deal with that when I am a little better"* – and we end up just pushing things that were always meant to be worked out, deeper within.

There is danger here. The more you press snooze, the more difficult it is to hear the alarm in your sleep. It becomes white noise, nothing. That's a scary place to get to in your heart – so numb to what you are feeling that you feel nothing at all.

Here is a truth I've learned: What is not processed makes no forward progress.

No forward progress. You just stay in bed. Asleep. Missing the world around you – your purpose.

You have to feel what you need to feel – and you can breathe through it. THROUGH implies progress.

The God of the universe did not breathe His very Spirit into you for you to sleep through your life.

He will sustain you, but are you giving Him the chance to help you thrive? Are you allowing God to work through you to bring His Life, Breath and Spirit to revive more people?

In scripture, sleep is a metaphor for death.

When Jairus' daughter was sick and passed away, Jesus showed up and said to the mourners,
"Stop the weeping! She isn't dead; she's only asleep."
Luke 8:52 (NLT)

He told her, *"My child, get up!" Luke 8:54 (NLT)*

Get up. Wake up. And she did! Jesus raised her from the dead. He woke her up.

I wonder if God wants to wake us up too. Maybe we have allowed our souls to fall asleep, and we need the resurrection power of Jesus to remind us of the Spirit with which we have been filled.
Wake up.

"Awake, O sleeper,
  rise up from the dead,
  and Christ will give you light."
  Ephesians 5:14 (NLT)

Maybe you're depressed and can't get yourself to move out of bed to even make yourself some cereal in the morning.

Or maybe you've experienced such a deep loss that you can't picture life working the same anymore.

Or maybe the disappointment of unrealized dreams has led you to stop trying. What is the point?

Or maybe the mistakes you have made feel too final, too messy. Your potential feels past repair. Broken.

We were not created to be defeated by sleep.

Our very bodies breathe in the middle of the night in our deepest sleep. The Spirit of the Living God can sustain you even in your seasons of deepest darkness.

You know there is an enemy to your soul. There is a pollution that threatens to choke you out – especially when your guard is down – especially when you are tired and worn out or sleeping.

You were designed to be able to fight. Your God can push out the darkness inside of you with the Light of His Spirit. Sin and death do not belong within someone who has been claimed by the Life-Giver – everything inside of you is set up to recognize the intrusion of darkness – you have to allow God to expel it from within you.

Do not submit to sleep. Process your pain. Face your sin. Awake, O Sleeper.

SLEEPWALKING
When I was little, I did all kinds of crazy stuff in my sleep.

Once I got ready for school in the middle of the night. I was convinced everyone in the house had overslept. More than once, I claimed my brother's bed as mine, which is funny because he slept on the top bunk of bunkbeds and I didn't even have a bunkbed. On one unfortunate occasion I was convinced the corner of our living room was, in fact, the bathroom and thought my parents were very mean for not letting me just do what I needed to do!

I remember one particular sleepover at a friend's grandparents' house. We showed up and my mom walked the house with my friend's grandma. The stairs in that house were grand – absolutely beautiful – and made of solid wood. There were 24 of them.

My mom was rightly afraid I would walk in my sleep and tumble down that massive staircase. She asked grandma so-and-so to put up a child gate. Or block the stairs with a table. Or lock me in my room. All effective.

This is the most subtle and terrifying danger I believe we face: looking and living as though we are awake while our soul is fast asleep.

It's dangerous because it is sometimes hard to detect. We can walk through life fast asleep, not truly taking anything in, not feeling, not processing. Some of us are convincing sleep-walkers.

Only those who know us best could identify the sleep beneath our steps. But asleep we are.

One of the biggest risks of sleepwalking is this: you may tumble down a big, sturdy flight of wood stairs.

There are spiritual obstacles – risks we cannot see while we are asleep. These staircases can cause us much pain. Think about the bruises, cuts and sore heads we receive in a good tumble. Then picture those bruises and cuts on your soul. No wonder we walk around wounded, unsure of how to heal.

SO MANY EMOTIONS
When I became a parent I had one giant fear: emotion.

My whole life, my family struggled to deal with our emotions. From chemical imbalances, to a lack of trust in Jesus, my upbringing didn't exactly teach me how to deal with what I was feeling appropriately, or even productively.

I was 28 before I realized I had struggled with anxiety my whole life.

It started with perfectionism as a little kid. My shoelaces had to be the exact same length. If I scratched my right arm, the left needed to be scratched as well. I needed control or I would lose it – we are talking giant child fits.

As I grew, so grew my inability to handle change in even the smallest form. As a teenager, I would fly off the handle if something didn't go as planned. I couldn't handle negative feedback or consequences without screaming, yelling and slamming doors.

My parents would often say to me, "Jenni, will you please resign as General Manager of the Universe?" The problem to me was I didn't think anyone else was doing that job! Who would take control of these situations so out of control? Who would

94

protect us? Who would fix this feeling?

I remember the feeling vividly. It was as if a dark mass was taking over my whole body. The darkness was strangely warm as it advanced – starting in my face, darkening my vision, growing to take the feeling from my hands and feet, the breath from my lungs and ultimately leaving no room inside me for the feelings I was feeling.

My emotions were too big for my body.
They clearly didn't belong here.

Then, in the first 2 years of my marriage I was plagued by a debilitating fear of the dark. Once the sun had gone down, I couldn't go outside without a large group of people. I could NEVER be home alone in the dark. I needed to have light always – everywhere.

My sweet, new husband had to be home before sunset or I would melt into a ball of unchecked emotion. Unable to deal with my feelings, I left them to him.

In those same years, we were trying to sort out our call to ministry and how to become leaders. I felt so ill-fit for God's work because I couldn't even keep my emotions in check. Fear was my leader.

That was the first time I went to counseling.

I was looking for something, or someone, to blame.

I wanted a diagnosis – an epiphany.
I wanted to live free.

What I received, sitting on that couch, was a responsibility.

The most important question I was ever taught to ask in an uncertain situation is this: What can you control?

The answer will vary. Sometimes, there is a lot I can control. Sometimes, there isn't.

Perhaps I made mistakes that led to my circumstance and I can fix them. I can apologize or right-set my behavior.

Are you drowning in debt? You can control your spending. Start by writing a budget. You can look for a new job to increase your income. You cannot control whether or not you get that job, though.

Are you sick? Maybe a loved one is sick. What can you control? You can get all the information out there about the illness you are facing. You can take the medication the doctor prescribes. Go to treatments. Rest. You cannot control your recovery.

Is your relationship broken? Romans 12:18 (NIV) says this: *If it is possible, as far as it depends on you, live at peace with everyone.* Is there someone you need to ask forgiveness from? Do you need to forgive? As far as it depends on you.

No matter the circumstance, there are things you can control and things you cannot. Often, the "things you cannot" will outnumber the "things you can" by a long shot. It's the gap between the two which leaves room for anxiety and fear to rush in. That is a gap which can be filled with something else. Let's fill it.

Here's what I do when I feel out of control: I grab a piece of paper. On the left, I write the things I can control. I always like to start there because it makes me feel like I have made some progress. Then on the right I write down the things I cannot control. I do this for everything in my life that overwhelms me.

The next step is so important.

If you're like me, the list on the right is scary. There are so many things we cannot control, and they are so tightly connected to people and things we love dearly. It's hard to admit we cannot control something when it means so much to us.

I take each thing on my list of "can nots" and bring it before Jesus – line by line. Systematically, I read each line, then I write the name of the one who is in control of all I am not in control of: Jesus. Fear – *Jesus*. What if – *Jesus*. I can't – *Jesus*.

I pray, *"Jesus, I can't control this, and I need your help."* Picture your own list. Maybe your list feels too overwhelming. Our submission will always lead to our peace. Pray that prayer for everything on your list and the words will ultimately lead to the feelings.

Our surrender to Jesus of the things we cannot control will open the door for the Holy Spirit to fill the gap between our "cans" and our "can nots". The best part is He has been waiting patiently for an invitation into the gap. Revelation 3:20 (NLT) says, *"Look! I stand at the door and knock. If you hear my voice and open the door, I will come in, and we will share a meal together as friends."*

We are not left to our list alone. Our responsibility is to right-think our responsibility. Is it possible that we are not nearly as powerful as we imagine?

You might be surprised at how your prayers will change through the process. Your surrender will grow to include prayers like, *"Your will be done, Jesus."* You may even pray, *"Even if it hurts, I will still praise you."*

And, don't be surprised when you begin to pray, *"Thank you Jesus for the circumstances outside my control because they have led me to a greater trust in you and your love for me."*

There's one more step.

That list on the left. The list of "can" controls. You'll have to ask Jesus to help you with those, too. Pick one and take a step forward. Don't rush into everything at once, but don't stay stuck. You have the great privilege of having a voice in your own life.

Write that budget. Make that appointment. Schedule that coffee date. Take ONE STEP.

With the action of the Holy Spirit inside of you and the action you can control in front of you, you may just realize that you have been breathing through your problem – that maybe your emotions are too big for your body, but not too big for your God.

Sometimes, that step is facing a fear. I want my kids to know how to process their emotions in a healthy way. I know they are still figuring out what their emotions are, but I don't ever want them to fear their emotions the way I did.

In my room is a big floral chair. I call it the "breathing chair." It was a great idea. When the kids are seemingly overwhelmed or frustrated or out of control, we can go sit together in my breathing chair. In the chair, we just sit together and breathe – in through our noses and out through our mouths. Jayne jumped right on it. She asks to go the breathing chair. Ryder, on the other hand? Let's just say he isn't an early adopter.

The point is this: I want my kids to know the power of breath in their physical and spiritual life. If they can learn to breathe now, they will be able to face anything later.

I will have exceeded my wildest dreams as a parent if my kids grow up knowing they can draw on the power of the same Spirit who created them – the Spirit who raised Christ from the dead – the Spirit who rescued their mom from the pit of despair. To know they can draw from that Spirit as naturally as they can take a breath.

Then they will know they can breathe through it – whatever it may be.

Are you ready to heal? Are you ready to feel the actual emotions you are feeling? Do not let them control you. Get help. Talk to someone you love and trust – who loves you and loves God. Take a breath. Let it out. Wake up from your sleep and breathe through it.

What is not processed makes no forward progress. Let's make some progress.

TIME TO BREATHE

Your turn:

WHO'S IN CONTROL

What you'll need:
- Paper/Journal
- Pen

What you'll do:
1. Start with drawing the line down the center of your paper.
2. On the left side, write the things you can control.
3. Then, on the right, write down the things you cannot control.
4. Go through your list on the right – for each one, write Jesus' name and give up your control by praying out loud. If you can only do one right now, that's great, but don't give up. Keep going and keep releasing as soon as you can get your spirit to that place.
5. Get back to that list you can control on the left. Pick one. Take one action. Then go back and do it again.
6. Realize you've been breathing through the emotions that overwhelm you.

IMPORTANT NOTE:
If you are facing emotions you do not understand and cannot control, please make an appointment with a counselor or your

doctor. You are not alone and you do not have to face what you are feeling alone. God created us to be in community, and some in our community are specifically equipped to help others make progress through healthy processing. Please don't remain isolated in your pain. Remember you have been called to a deep, full life.

The God of the universe did not breathe His very Spirit into you for you to sleep through your life.

in the running and in the resting
and in the racing and in the calm.

RUNNING

Did you know that the average adult takes 12-20 breaths per minute while resting? That jumps up to 40-50 while exercising!

I like to run on the track at the YMCA. Outside weather is unpredictable in the PNW . . . and I like to people watch . . . or in this case, listen.

Have you ever noticed how many kinds of breathers there are at the gym? Picture yourself with me, running the indoor track at the YMCA. I usually notice at least four types of breathers while people-listening. I have a theory that all of us are at least one of these types. You'll have to self-diagnose:

The mouth breather. This is the guy who you can literally hear from the opposite side of the track. You just move over without looking because he might as well have tapped you on the shoulder with his absurdly loud mouth breathing. Now, I will offer an explanation which may help out the mouth breather. Maybe he has a cold? His nose is so stuffed up that he has to get it all in and out through his mouth. But wouldn't you just NOT run while you are sick? Maybe I'm just not committed enough.

The mouse. I can't even tell if this person is breathing at all. It looks like they are working hard, like, I see the sweat. Good job, lady. I'm just concerned for your respiration. *"Excuse me, can someone keep an eye out for the woman in the "hear me roar" tank over there? I'm not hearing her roar and I'm thinking she could be a fall risk."*

The labor breather. Hee-Hee-Hoo. Hee-Hee–Hoo. You know this friend took a super fulfilling mind and body class (which I am all about) or got confused after Lamaze and stuck with a pattern that works. You do you, labor breather. I'mma put in my headphones.

The albuterol. Alright. Spoiler. This is me. I love to run, but I have exercise-induced asthma, which is probably just code for OUT-OF-SHAPE-NEED-MORE-EXERCISE, but my doctor was too nice. I've trained and trained – in through your nose – out through your mouth, but still . . . 1 mile in and my arms are above my head and I'm taking a walking lap with my inhaler.

Arms above my head. Does that feel a bit like a cry for help to anyone else? It's like the universal "my car hood is up, so I need a mechanic" but for out of shape runners.

My chest is compressed, the pressure is too much, I have to make room for the air – arms up.
Breathe in.

The worst part of getting to that place is that the breathing hurts. You almost have to go slower, use more care. It's not about running slower, it's about focusing more on breathing.

When we are active, our hearts work harder. It's just more difficult to get the oxygen from the air. It was explained to me like this: If I'm holding a candy jar and slowly passing you by with it, you can grab large handfuls of candy with little difficulty. If I begin to swing the candy jar past you faster and faster, the task of grabbing candy becomes harder and harder.

That's what our lungs experience when we are active. It's harder and harder to get the oxygen from the air, but the air is still there.

Did you catch that? The air is still there. You have access to the Spirit of God, even when you are running hard through life. We have to look to see that nothing about God has changed in our moments of running. He is still as available as He has always been.

We need to adjust our approach to receiving Him when we are running hard. The danger is in neglecting to train to receive God when running. We have to learn to take breaths at a new pace. To take breaks, and to trust that God is with us in the running. Fear can step in to steal our confidence in God. Breathlessness is terrifying. We don't have to get to that place, even when we are working hard.

Training for a run, you'll learn, it is difficult at first. It hurts to breathe because your body isn't yet prepared to pull more oxygen. Your heart is beating so fast. The candy jar is moving too fast.

As you train you'll begin to notice changes. Your muscles will feel stronger. Your heart, a muscular organ, will strengthen and be able to sustain its rate over time and varied activity. One of my friends who runs endurance races shared with me that her resting heartrate is 65 bpm. When she is running it only increases to 75-90 bpm! Her candy jar of oxygen isn't moving by nearly as fast as mine is when I am running, out of shape.

For her running isn't nearly as painful as it is for a person who has not trained. She can sustain her pace for long distances because her body is able to receive the oxygen it needs. Of course there will come a time when her muscles need a rest, we cannot push forever, but her body has adapted. She is able to withstand much more activity and exertion because of her training.

Could our spirits adapt to withstand much more as we learn to receive God while running hard after His purposes?

Paul says to run the race to win . . .

Don't you realize that in a race everyone runs, but only one person gets the prize? So run to win! All athletes are disciplined in their training. They do it to win a prize that will fade away, but we do it for an eternal prize. So I run with purpose in every step. I am not just shadowboxing. I discipline my body like an athlete, training it to do what it should . . . 1 Corinthians 9:24-27 (NLT)

You have to discipline your body. Why?

So you don't break. So you don't pass out. So you don't collapse on the sidelines of the race or experience injury that can threaten your ability to race at all.

This means to take breaks when you need to. Use a training plan. Plot your course but schedule your rest.

Raise your arms when your breathing is labored and you need help. Take a walking lap. Purpose in every step. Recovery is a worthy purpose.

Learn to receive the right amount of breath at the right time while you are running.

We must learn to discipline our Spirits.

Run fast. Run hard. Jesus said we would do even greater things than He did on this Earth – but you can't do it if you are collapsed on the side of the track.

Life in the Spirit takes intentionality and awareness of your soul's condition.

Raise your hand. I need more oxygen. I need help.

Take your rest. I need to build up my muscles and stretch so my muscles can receive more oxygen while they are in use.

Run with discipline. Plan your pace and keep to it.

Run hard. Breathe deep.

RAISE YOUR HAND

So, what do we do when we are running hard through life and we face an emotion we don't understand? We've learned to breathe and we are committed to making progress, but now there is resistance.

This is when fear can step in to cause us to distrust our access to the Spirit. What do we do when we feel like something is keeping us from breathing while living out our life in the Spirit? This is where you raise your hand, saying I need help.

How do you process what you are feeling, naturally?

Just like the four types of breathers, I tend to see four types of processors. (These are not scientific by any means, just my observations.)

The mouth breather.
This is the verbal processor – who processes A LOT.

The mouth breather has a hard time choosing who to process with, so they just open their mouths all the time – to everyone.

There is something to be said about the transparency of the mouth breather. They don't really care if you know about all their dirty laundry, but they also don't really care if you WANT to know.

The danger here is oversaturation. If you talk about what you are facing with everyone, then no one is really "safe". It's hard to get good advice from 20 people – but 3? Three seems right. If you poll 20 people, you are likely to find the answer you want in that group. If you ask 3 people you trust, chances are the honest answer will become much more clear.

Jenni, I'm a mouth breather, do I need to change?

Maybe. The word I would use is adjust. Be more picky. Verbal process a lot, but with fewer people. You can't change the way your brain processes, but you can learn discipline. Who are the 3 people in your life who love you and love God? Talk to them.

Don't lose your God-given ability to share openly what is happening in your heart. This is a gift that many wish they had, so don't waste it.

The mouse.
This is the silent sufferer.

The mouse almost never shares their struggles. So, rarely do they process outside of their own mind. There is a tendency to be a stuffer here. This silent processor tends to hang on to their emotions and bury them deep. Avoidance, forgetfulness, anything to not feel what you are feeling.

Author, Lysa TerKeurst, writes in her book *Unglued* about 2 types of stuffers. The first is the stuffer who collects rocks. You might define this is passive aggressive. You are just watching all the hard things around you and allowing them to pile up – building walls you hide behind and ammunition to throw later when the stuffing gets too difficult.

The second type of stuffer is the one who implodes. The pressure gets to be too much and instead of exploding, they fall apart. Their heart, resolve and dreams disintegrate into tiny pieces – unrecognizable on the floor.

There is wisdom in silence – so many people don't know how to just be quiet. Scripture tells us to be still. Sitting and listening is a skill the mouse has nailed. How I wish I had more silent moments in my life.

To you who are quiet, I want to encourage you. Don't isolate. Find one person you are able to share with – just one. Do you have one safe person in your life?

Maybe your answer is no. At the very least buy a journal. Begin to write down how you feel. One of my favorite things about journaling is watching how, as I write, the Holy Spirit meets me on the pages. He will answer you and direct you as you open your heart to His leading.

The labor breather.
One of my favorite things about this processor is their commitment to the process.

I have a friend who must go through every step of a process. Step by step. Every time. Over and over.

Can I tell you that I am not patient enough for that?

But my friend craves the process – she needs the steps to feel like she is in control. And, maybe that's the danger with this type of processor. Do you struggle with control in your problems? Do you try to manage, shift and turn the situation you are facing to fit the mold of what you have the ability to handle?

Life doesn't have a bow on it. Problems stay without bridges. We have to learn to breathe through it – whatever it may be.

At times, your best action is to let go of what you feel like you need to control.

Picture your life like a hand. When you close your fist tight around the things you love – your dreams, your process, your plan – then everything is safe from what lies outside of your fist. The unfortunate outcome of a closed-fist approach to life is this: in trying to keep out the bad, you make it impossible to receive the good. A closed fist can receive nothing – good or bad.

An open hand may be more vulnerable, but it is also more available. We cannot control what comes into our lives, but we can control how we respond to God in the midst of it.

Here's my encouragement: Live your life with an open hand. Watch how the Holy Spirit interrupts your process to show Himself to be the very best Protector and most generous Provider.

The albuterol.
Sometimes, we are so sick it actually can't get better

without help.

Are you hurting, broken and unable to breathe? Are you stuck, unable to process what you are facing? Friend, get help.
Sometimes our problems really are too big.

Whoever said that God would not give us more than we can bear did not read well. The scripture says *we will not be tempted beyond what we can bear (1 Corinthians 10:13)*. If I am honest, everything is too much for me without the leadership and love of my God.

This world is so very broken, and I am so very broken. It's hard for broken to fix broken, and I don't think God is asking us to.

We actually need God. That is not wrong, it is true. It is a gift to need Him.

We need community.
We need family.
We need shelter.
We need medicine.
We need sleep.
We need food.

Need is not weakness. It is our design.

We were designed from the beginning to need our great Healer, our great Creator, our great Resurrector.

Ask for help. You don't have to be your own hero – Jesus has already filled that place in your life. Let God lead you toward health and healing.

TAKE YOUR REST
Our God is a God of rhythms.

When He created us, He put the rhythm of breathing into our physical bodies to point to our constant need for the Holy Spirit to fill us.

He also created a rhythm to time. Remember Genesis Chapter 1 (and the very beginning of chapter 2)? In the creation poem, each day had a purpose – a beginning and an end. I like to think this example is where Paul got the encouragement he wrote to the Corinthians of purpose in every step. On the seventh day, God's purpose was to rest.

On the seventh day God had finished his work of creation, so he rested from all his work. And God blessed the seventh day and declared it holy, because it was the day when he rested from all his work of creation. Genesis 2:2-3 (NLT)

I do not usually associate rest with power. Do you? I desire power, and tend to avoid rest. I'll go out on a limb and assume I'm not the only one. We want to have control. We yearn to design our own destiny. We dream. We hope. We plan.

Maybe, like me, you fear that if you slow down or stop for even a moment you will miss some cosmic happening which was meant to propel your life to what it was always meant to be.

It's a fine line we walk between healthy ambition and idolatry of self.

Idolatry is any replacement of God in my life.

Idolatry of self. I think that's the core issue in me when I refuse to rest. That idolatry is sin.

When I believe my ultimate purpose can be thwarted by my action or inaction, I misunderstand the true power of God.

When I assume, and then live like, my purpose is dependent on me – I am putting myself in the place of God. It's self-worship.

God's purposes are always and only dependent on God. When I take time to seek what I truly desire, I know it is to fulfill God's purposes for me, not my own. My guess is that is you desire this deeply as well.

But, when I don't give my heart the chance to slow down to receive more of God – I can easily confuse my plans for His.

I love Jesus, so over time, my plans can look suspiciously like His. The fine line is a dangerous thing to walk.

The only way to make that line more defined is to spend more time resting and receiving.

Have you seen the old cartoon of Wile E. Coyote and The Road Runner? I remember one specific exchange in which the Coyote turned a sign in the opposite direction Road Runner wanted to go. Because Road Runner was moving so quickly and not stopping, he ended up half a world in the wrong direction.

I don't want to waste time backtracking when I could be running hard after God's purpose for me.

I don't want any of us to miss what God wants to give. We are no good to God depleted, or in the completely wrong place.

So, we stop. We rest. We receive.

Then, we run our hardest for the Glory of God.

RUN WITH DISCIPLINE
This is one of the most important aspects to a spiritually healthy life.

No one loves the word discipline. If you're like me, it draws to your mind scenes of writing line after line of "I will not talk while others are talking" in second grade. Or perhaps you picture summer afternoons wasted while completing the very worst set of chores in the house. Maybe you have a military background and discipline is life.

117

Committed routine. Hard training.

Most of the time, scripture uses a word like discipline to refer to God's discipline of us as His children. Most of us would be in agreement that children should be disciplined (as a verb) to become healthy adults.

Why? Because discipline is training.

In our church, we teach that the highest goal of parenting is to transfer your kids' dependence on you to a dependence on God.

We have to train to depend on God.

There was an age at which you had to be reminded to shower, brush your teeth, go to bed at a decent hour, set your alarm, make it on time (or at least close to on time) to your commitments.

Then, there comes an age at which each of us should be disciplined enough in our own lives that we can handle those healthy undertakings on our own.

Discipline is a sign of deep love. From a parent to a child, discipline shows a desire for the child to grow into an independent person, full of purpose and ability. In you, as an independent adult, self-discipline shows you carry an actionable belief that you are full of purpose and ability.

You are full of purpose and ability. You can run hard and fast after that purpose because of the ability God has placed inside of you. God calls you His Masterpiece. You are worth the effort.

We must train. Our God who loves us is waiting to lead us.

Remember what Paul says in 1 Corinthians 9: *So run to win! All athletes are disciplined in their training.*

I have a friend who loves to run crazy races. I'm talking the extravagantly crazy ones. He has completed an Ironman, and actually plans to run more. He's insane.

An Ironman is a race including a 2.4-mile swim, a 112-mile bicycle ride and a marathon . . . all in a row . . . without stopping.

You don't get to the finish line of a race like that without major training.

For over a year, he would wake up early and ride his bike on a seriously long route, go to the gym to run on the machine and then cool off with a ridiculous swim.

On many occasions during that training season our friends were all hanging out and would notice he was missing. We would find him asleep in one of the bedrooms at 5 p.m. – it didn't matter whose house we were at. He was training hard.

I also remember the man could not stop eating. He was starving all the time, but in the best shape of his life.

The harder he trained, the more rest he needed and the more food he craved.

That's what training does. That is what training in our spiritual lives will do when we allow our spirits to be disciplined.

We will need the rest modeled by our God. Our hunger for the things of God will be insatiable.

You won't be able to get enough good teaching, books, time reading scripture, worship music. This is about filling our Spirits with the things of God so we are led from a place of fullness and purpose.

Any good athlete sets a training schedule. Time is the most difficult thing to wrangle in our busy world. Set a time to allow the Holy Spirit to fill you. He will fill you with encouragement, peace and joy. When you are ready, you can run hard as you are propelled by the love and purpose of our God.

TIME TO BREATHE

The following is an important spiritual practice. You must allow God to be Lord of your time. There are tons of physical benefits to setting a good sleep schedule, waking up at the same time every day and planning great meals. There is spiritual benefit to even that basic physical rhythm. It will create space to receive God in places which used to be filled with busyness, worry and fast food runs.

I know lots of people who are night owls and love to spend their time with Jesus at night. I will admit I am a morning person, so the schedule I will suggest includes Jesus time in the morning. I am partial to the idea of, before everything else, letting the Holy Spirit influence my agenda for the day. As with all these exercises, the following is only a suggestion to lead to your own practice:

TRAINING SCHEDULE

What you'll need:
- Calendar
- Phone or Alarm clock
- Sleep tracker app (possibly)

What you'll do:
1. Decide how much sleep leaves you feeling refreshed (try a sleep tracking app). I read

that most adults need 6 or 9 hrs. of sleep to be well rested.

2. When do you have to start getting ready for work, head to the gym or begin your day with kids in the morning? Give yourself at least an hour before your first task of day. Is that 7 a.m.? 6 a.m.? 5 a.m.? For me, 5 a.m. is the best time to begin with. Set your alarm for your new wake-up time.

3. Work backward from your wakeup time, marking the amount of hours you need to sleep. That's your new bedtime. Yes, bedtime. Can I tell you this is the hardest part for me? Bedtime may be the most difficult and the most important spiritual practice in my life. The next day truly begins the night before.

4. Do you need to set your coffee maker to brew or set out your clothes? Do you have 'your place' ready for the next morning? Set your new rhythm so your morning can belong to Jesus.

5. Go to bed on time.

6. Get out of bed when your alarm goes off.

7. Meet with Jesus and let His Spirit lead your time with Him in 'your place'.

8. Repeat every day. You are in training. We are all in training. Training is difficult, and so rewarding.

CIRCUMSTANCES

---

my whole body hurts.

HOLDING YOUR BREATH

The soccer bus was my favorite.

We told stories, shared secrets and deodorant we didn't yet need. It was junior high and the best possible thing we could experience in life was an away game.

I felt so proud wearing my jersey to school, sporting the note from Coach Scott to get me out of 5th and 6th period . . . because we had a game.

I played center mid, a position which Richard says is what people who don't play soccer say they played . . . but I was pretty good at it. It came easy for me.

So did making friends. For the most part. My soccer friends were especially competitive – as you can imagine. Most of the teams we played were located across a bridge that is a little longer than a mile – the Tacoma Narrows.

The game we played on the bus ride was simple, yet challenging.

Every player would have to touch one of the screws that held the bus windows in place, while keeping their feet from touching the floor and, of course, holding their breath across the whole bridge.

It was a rite of passage. As an adult, I still have the urge to pick up my feet and hold my breath when I drive across that bridge. Of course, I recognize feet are important to keeping a car going, so I refrain . . . although, there is this handy invention called cruise control. It both saves my feet and my pocketbook. *("Sorry officer, I was just writing a book in my head – no, I had no idea I was going 80 m.p.h. – yes, I do have insurance, and time to go to traffic court . . .")*

I was driving my kids and some family friends to the zoo the other day when my 12-year-old "niece" began bragging about how long she could hold her breath. I watched (safely from my peripheral vision) as she held her breath all the way across that well-marked bridge.

We've seen magicians tackle crazy feats and divers prove their lung capacity. Bored teenagers and junior high soccer players for generations have tried to see how long they can hold their breath.

I had a friend whose toddler started a really scary response to her emotions. She started holding her breath when she was mad. She would just sit down on the ground and stop breathing. She even passed out from withholding air from her tiny lungs.

At that first workout class I went to, I remember my instructor reminding us over and over again, "breathe" – "don't hold your breath".

Maybe you've watched a really intense movie or news story unfolding, and as you yearn for the tension to subside you realize you have been holding your breath awaiting the resolution.

I wonder if we do this with our souls and circumstances, too.

Maybe not intentionally, but do you ever find yourself holding your breath?

Life gets busy, kids get demanding and careers start to sky rocket . . . and you can't remember the last time you took a breath, let alone released one.

Someone hurt you, years ago, and that bitterness is just sitting in your spirit.

You believe life is unfair. You have worked hard and nothing seems to go your way. You are angry at God. This feeling is building and building with no release.

You were right. They were wrong. The wound is real and unjust, but the withholding forgiveness is going to destroy you.

You have been waiting for the tension to subside or for the feelings to change or to win the competition and you realize the only thing that is happening for sure is that you are losing your ability to live.

The strangest thing about holding your breath is how near we are to the relief. It's as close as breathing.

We release what we have been holding on to and receive what God has been trying to give us all along.

It's a choice to hold your breath. And it is a choice to breathe. It takes discipline. It takes trust. We hold on to control when we choose not to breathe, but what do we lose?

You aren't winning any competitions for being self-sufficient in this life. Too much self-sufficiency is self-destructive.

Make a choice to stop depriving yourself of the oxygen your soul desperately needs.

Set a time. When will you take a breath? When will

you sit down with a friend for dinner and talk about how God is at work in your life? Oxygen.

When will you take that hike with your kids – see them grow and progress – hear their questions and ask your own? Get away from the noise and listen for God's voice? Oxygen.

When will you pour a cup of coffee in the early hours of the morning, watch the sunrise and allow yourself to be filled with the second chances that God has built into the very fabric of creation? Oxygen.

When will you stop holding your breath?

Maybe you find yourself unable to breathe at all – and you are trying to. You are not alone, and we all need help sometimes.

Is your soul in an emergency state? There is a way through even the most dire of circumstances.

911

When our son was 8 days old, he stopped breathing.

Not for just a second. The child was purple. We were brand new parents and had no idea what to do. I was about to lose my son before I even got to know him. Too many of my friends have faced this type of tragedy. My heart breaks.

I was fast asleep and something woke Richard – he says now it was a gurgling sound. Remember . . . this is 12-Alarm-Richard, who never wakes up . . . Jesus was clearly with us that night.

We tried to see if there was something blocking his airway, but his tiny mouth was fused shut – we couldn't even pry it open.

Richard yelled to me to call 911.

> *911: 911, what's your emergency*

> *ME: My baby isn't breathing, he's purple. He's so small.*

> *911: We're sending an ambulance. Do you know CPR?*

> *ME: _____*
> *(Ambulance. They think my baby needs an ambulance. We might not make it through this. He might never breathe again. I can't help him. I can't help me. No one can help me. They are too far. Ambulances take too long. What if we can't fix him?)*

> *911: Ma'am, do you know CPR?*

I handed the phone to Richard and I prayed harder than I had prayed before and have prayed since – that the Breath of God would fill my sweet baby's lungs again. That life would reach his bones. That his days would be marked with future, not memory.

The 911 operator walked Richard through infant CPR over the phone and on the 5th or 6th compression, Ryder began small shallow breaths. Each inhale brought his purple back to pink and his life back from the grips of death.

It was the compressions that ultimately saved Ryder's life.

Have you taken a CPR class? In my first CPR class, they taught us to give 2 breaths – 5 compressions – 2 breaths – 5 compressions – and so on. That pattern has changed many times over the years.

Now, professionals, like my respiratory therapist friend say to focus on the compressions.

In hospitals and medical training, there is a gauge which measures the out-put of carbon dioxide from a patient receiving compressions. A compression must result in at least 10 cmH20 of C02 releasing to be effective. [*SIDE NOTE: There is such a thing as being 'too effective'; remember that our bodies register the need to breathe by the level of carbon dioxide they sense. We need the in and the out.*]

Professionals can tell if their compressions are effective by checking to ensure enough pollution is leaving the patient's system. If not, then the blood isn't flowing, the heart isn't functioning and clean oxygen isn't getting to the lungs.

The pollution must get out, so life can regain

its power.

I wonder if some of the circumstances we face in life which shock us and knock the wind out of us, were designed to get rid of pollution we didn't realize resided in our souls.

Maybe it takes a life-compression to get the life flowing in us again.

After Ryder regained his breath, we spent the next 2 days in the hospital on seizure watch. They found nothing wrong with little Ryder. I can still feel it. Sitting in the small, square hospital room with my eyes glued to the oxygen gauge. 98%. 96%. 99%. 94%. 91% . . . 97%.

I watched and prayed that the oxygen would flow into his blood to sustain his life. Any negative fluctuation of that percentage sent me into a spiral of worry.

I wanted him to be filled with breath. Full of life. As close to 100 percent as possible.

Friends, our Good Father wants the same for us.

He wants us to be filled with His Breath. *And because you belong to him, the power of the life-giving Spirit has freed you from the power of sin that leads to death. Romans 8:2 (NLT).*

We are free when we are filled.

Breathe in the Spirit of the Living God. Embrace your freedom.

I hadn't thought very seriously about calling 911 until I had to do it. Looking back, I had this strange realization – it never, even once, occurred to me that someone would not answer my call.

I never thought, *"I hope they answer."* I just called for help, and expected the help to come.

Isn't it strange that we have such confidence in a person on the other end of a phone call, but struggle to believe that God will be there when we call?

Prayer is our 911 call, but better – because we don't have to be in an emergency to open up the conversation.

Jeremiah 33:3 (NIV) says this: *"Call to me and I will answer you and tell you great and unsearchable things you do not know."*

That is the voice of your God saying to you,
"I'm here."
"I will answer."
"I will lead you to greater truth and deeper life than you could ever imagine."
"It's better than you know."

Our God will not stop until every bit of His love fills your soul – until you are overflowing into the whole world around you, because there is beyond more than enough for you.

Breathe in.

There is resurrection power in every breath.

DEAD THINGS DON'T STAY DEAD
Have you ever seen someone who has passed away? That question may bring up some really difficult memories for you. It does for me.

I was 19 years old and engaged to be married in less than two weeks. *(Yes, we were married as infants.)*

My dad called, "Jenni, Papah is the hospital. It's a bad case of pneumonia. He should be fine, but Grandmommy wants some company".

Papah *(pronounced Pa-paw)* and Grandmommy are my dad's parents. My dad was an only child, so they followed us everywhere we ever moved. I grew up with them seconds away at all times.

Papah and I were especially close. My dad inherited Papah's humor and I inherited Dad's. The three of us were a mess, albeit a funny one.

My then fiancé, Richard, and I showed up at the hospital to hang around with the family and entertain Grandmommy, who worried a lot.

We were there for probably 3 hours while the

doctors performed some tests and a low-risk procedure.

The whole family was waiting, playing games in the waiting room when we hear over the loud speaker, *"Code Blue, Room ____."*

I don't even remember the room number, because my heart stopped when I heard the words "code blue."

Granted, we were in the hospital and announcements like that happened all the time, but I just knew.

It seemed like we all knew. The next 10 minutes felt like 2 hours.

A doctor came in to ask for my dad to step outside with him for a moment.

When Dad walked back in, Grandmommy broke down. Papah was gone.

His lungs and weak heart couldn't handle the stress of his illness and just gave up.

Dad asked me if I wanted to go say goodbye to him. I didn't. But I did anyway.

I don't think it is possible for the room to have been 10 degrees colder than the hallway outside, but it sure felt that way to me.

He lay there on the hospital bed in silence. I walked over to him – it was just the two of us in the room. I guess, just the one of us. He was so still. His skin was ashy. I didn't touch him, but I watched him for a few minutes.

I saw nothing. I heard nothing. He had been there and now he was gone. I couldn't get past the strangeness of his still chest. No up and down. No inhale, no exhale.

Death had stolen his breath.

Ultimate breathlessness.

What do you do with that? How do we face death? It feels so final, so powerful. Death steals the gift of breath away. Is all this work of living Spirit-filled and full of Breath pointless in the end?

I remembered the words of Jesus in that moment in that too-cold hospital room, "he's asleep."

He's asleep. The God I serve belittled and embarrassed death by the Resurrection of Jesus. Death is only sleeping. What seemed to be final, so powerful minutes before was rendered powerless by sacrificial love – on that day at Calvary, and in that hospital room, in my mourning.

Death cannot defeat God. Over and over again in scripture, death is defeated. In small ways and in big ways, death is cheated of its prize.

Have you noticed this theme in Scripture?
That dead things just have a habit of being raised
back to life?

One of my favorite pictures of this is in the story of
Ezekiel. You can look it up later, but I'll tell you
what happens. *(Ezekiel, Chapter 37)*

Ezekiel was a prophet of God to the Jewish people
exiled in Babylon. Judah was taken by Babylon in
598 B.C.

King Nebuchadnezzar, who I like to call "Neb",
defeated Jerusalem, and then took close to 10,000
people into exile back to Babylon. He brought with
him the best, brightest and richest; leaving the poor,
sick and elderly to their desolation and devastation.

When the people arrived in Babylon, they were
taught the ways of Babylon. They were instructed
to forget their home, their language and their God.

Can you see how Ezekiel had a hopeless job?
Prophet of God in Babylon, sent to remind the
people of God's goodness even though everything
about their lives has been ripped from them.

Years of tradition – gone, dead.
Family they loved – gone, dead.
Hope for a free life – gone, dead.
Their language – gone, dead.
Their very names were taken from them (remember
Daniel? His name was changed to Belteshazzar;

from God is Judge to a name honoring a Babylonian God).

Ezekiel walks onto that scene, in exile himself, proclaiming that God is still alive and well, active among them.

Do you see it? We are all in exile. We belong in the presence of God. Here, there is pain – confusing, unexplainable pain. Loss is rampant – some of us have experienced it so deeply it is hard to believe life still exists.

Friends, it takes one voice. One person willing to stand up to say that God is Good in my life. Despite my exile, my hope remains. My hope is in the knowledge that my Good God will come for me . . . is coming for me . . . that my Good God has already come for me.

Much like Ezekiel went with the people into exile to proclaim the Goodness of God, Jesus entered our exile here. God became *a human being (Philippians 2:5-11, NLT)*. He came and *made his home among us (John 1:14, NLT)*.

He made His home among us. Aren't we all searching for our home? Our God moved in to the neighborhood. Lived, loved, died and rose again to new life to show us that our Home has always been wherever God is. And because of the Holy Spirit, God is in us.

Our world is full of people who have lost or have never known their home. Maybe you have been desperate to find the foundation you can stand on to face the world around you. Trusting in the name of Jesus and receiving His Life-giving Spirit is the only way I know to find the strength to face the world of loss around us.

The Jewish people had lost their home – they had lost their hope. And, like us when we are in that place of hopelessness, they needed a message. A voice to call out to them.

It would take an incredibly strong message to bring those lost, hurting people back to belief in a Good God – or really, a God at all.

God gave Ezekiel that message in Ezekiel, Chapter 37. He says the Spirit of God carried him to a valley filled with dry bones.

God asks Ezekiel as he is looking over a valley filled with human skeletons (this is PG-13 stuff) if the prophet believed the bones could become living people again.

[SIDE NOTE – and I love this one . . . There is another time when that phrase "living people" or "living person" is found . . . Remember? Genesis 2:7 – God breathed His Spirit, and the man became a living person. Same God – same methods – same life . . . End side note]

So Ezekiel tells God that only He, the Life-Giver

can answer that question.

God tells Ezekiel to speak to the bones. As he obeys, right before his eyes, the bones put themselves back together – wrapped with flesh and muscles.

Then there is an important pause –

a conjunction . . . the word "but."

. . . but they still had no breath in them.
Ezekiel 37:8b (NLT)

God tells Ezekiel to call the wind to breathe life into the bones.

Ezekiel calls to the wind and the bones became LIVING PEOPLE.

Ezekiel saw broken, dry, dead bones – who had lost their breath, their life, take it up again – in the way God has always intended.

They weren't just a little dead – they had been dead for years. Bones that were completely broken, scattered. Like the people of Israel, they were scattered and divided, hopeless. Many years past hoping that God would show up. Many years past belief in a rescue. Their hearts and their dreams were dead.

The wind came and breath came into their bodies. They all

came to life and stood up on their feet—a great army.
Ezekiel 37:10 (NLT)

As they stood before God, He said to them, "O my people, I
will open your graves of exile and cause you to rise again."
Ezekiel 37:12 (NLT)

I will cause you to rise again. You are not too far
gone. There is no such thing. Death is not the end
of the story.

You see, dead things don't stay dead.

This narrative is written throughout ALL of
scripture, not just after Jesus rises. Death is cheated.
Death is defeated.

- Aaron's staff – dry, dead wood – blossoms
  before the Pharaoh. Not just life, but
  beauty. *(Numbers, Chapter 17)*
- The widow and her son are met by the
  prophet Elijah in a famine and drought –
  "we are making our last meal." God does a
  miracle, and they experience plenty, life
  sustained when it should have been lost.
  (1 Kings, Chapter 17)
- Shadrach, Meshach, and Abednego are
  thrown into an actual furnace, so hot it
  killed the guards who threw them in – and
  they emerge alive, not even smelling of
  smoke. Fire and death, cheated.
  (Daniel, Chapter 3)

- Jonah lives in the belly of a fish at the bottom of the ocean. Life sustained, even at rock bottom. *(Jonah, Chapters 1-2)*
- Daniel made friends with a pride of lions. Death in submission to Life. *(Daniel, Chapter 6)*
- And this – the dry bones come alive – not just flesh walking around void of spirit, but fully alive with breath provided by the God who created the wind. *(Ezekiel, Chapter 37)*

We were not intended to walk through our life as a sack of flesh and bones, but fully alive in Christ. We have the Spirit of the Living God in us – the one who has always had the upper hand on sin, death and evil.

Is the death in you being called to life? Are you being revived today? This life is a continuous, progressive revival.

I love to go to places I can feel the wind – high mountains, the ocean, open trails. When I feel the wind, I am reminded there is more breath than I know – there is more life than I know.

The power of the wind speaks the truth to my heart that Breath doesn't run out. Life doesn't run out, not true Life. Because even dry bones can live when they are filled with Breath from the wind.

God told Ezekiel to call the wind – to speak Life

over the dry bones.

Once we have been filled with life, nothing by life will do, and it is our responsibility to share this message of hope. Just try to keep it inside . . . you can't. Because seeing death conquered by life isn't a story you keep to yourself.

If you've stood in the valley of dry bones and seen the power of the wind – the rhythm of this life is permanently altered as you are no longer slave to loss and pain and death. You know you have the God who made the wind speaking into you.

Who is God asking you to call the wind for? Who can you speak the Life-giving power of God's Spirit into today?

I dare you. Watch how God sends the wind – and how that wind will revive your own soul in the process.

BUT WHAT ABOUT THE DEAD THINGS?
I know.

There are some things in my life that still feel dead. Some bridges from where I am to the other side of my circumstance which are still broken. Gone. I am still facing bridgeless places.

What do we do with bridgeless places?

Most of the time when I want to know what to do

and I have no idea, I look at what Jesus did.

There is a story about Jesus I love. His friend, Lazarus, is sick and he's asked to go and heal him. He makes plans to go, but hangs out where He is a few more days. We read later that Jesus knew His friend had already died. At that moment, He knew that His friend had stopped breathing and was being buried. He knew that Lazarus' sisters were in mourning. He knew that the community was rallying around this family experiencing deep and true loss. Knowing all of that, here is what He says:

"Our friend Lazarus has fallen asleep; but I am going there to wake him up." John 11:11 (NLT)

But, I am going there to WAKE. HIM. UP.

Lazarus was dead for 4 days before Jesus got to him. When He showed up, Lazarus' sister, Jesus' friend Martha, was angry – *"if only you had been here, Jesus . . ."*

Have you ever felt like that? Jesus – if only you had stepped in. If only you did your work in my life, I would not have this problem. I would not be stuck. I would be able to breathe.

Jesus said to her, "I am the resurrection and the life. The one who believes in me will live, even though they die. John 11:25 (NLT)

This is our God.

The God who makes dead things alive.

Lazarus rises. Death is physically defeated in this moment. But first, death looked like it was winning for 4 days.

4 days. 4 days that probably felt like an eternity for his sisters who were mourning. 4 days full of denial, anger, discontentment and such sadness. 4 days looking for some way, any way, for this tragedy to not be reality.

Can you possibly be content to allow something to be dead? Can you be content to let your circumstance go unresolved. It would take deep confidence, that in the arms of our God, dead things don't stay dead.

Can you let go of the control of whatever you are holding tightly to? Can you let it pass away, and still believe that God loves you – that God is with you – that God is for you?

I have spent so much of my life trying to revive things which have been lost – pouring all my energy into chest compressions over a corpse of a dream. I've begged God to keep my way, my dream, my plan alive. But, I wonder in this way if we have forgotten a most foundational truth.

Resurrection demands death.

God heals things, yes, and we praise Him for it.

But to raise something to new life, it must die first.

I love the story of Lazarus because there is no way that after four days his resurrection could be anything other than the miracle it was.

I wonder if we are trying, desperately, to hang on to our way, our plan, our dream . . . and God is just waiting for us to let go to do His miracle.
We want the miracle.
We want the control.

Which do you want more?

The best part about worshipping Jesus is that He not only resurrected, but He is the resurrection – did you catch that in His statement to Martha?

Jesus is the Resurrection. We can't fully serve Jesus without believing that nothing is too dead for Him to raise to New Life. We can't fully serve Jesus without believing in the resurrecting power of His Spirit.

The existence of death is a result of our sinful existence.

The existence of Life precedes death. Life is the launch point from which all of Creation sprung forth. Death is only a temporary absence of life. Temporary.

Our God promises that He is making all things

new. Nothing will be as it is. Dead things won't stay dead – they can't.

Death was intended to be the ultimate Breath-taker, but when faced with the Life-giver, it cannot hope to stand.
Life wins, because Jesus lives. Just like snuffing out a candle does not mean that fire does not exist, the existence of death does not mean that life is gone. Life cannot be defeated by death.

There is always more breath because there is always more of God.

Resurrection demands death, yes. But, it also defeats it. Death can come time and time again, but Resurrection will follow.

God can always bring life. Life was created before death, defeats death, and will live long beyond the memory of death.

Deep breaths of God will wash away the evidence that death ever was as our God makes all things new.

What about the dead things? Our God is breathing, even now, raising them to Life.

TIME TO BREATHE

WHO AM I?

What you'll need:
- Paper/Journal
  (if you don't want to write in this book)
- Pen

What you'll do:
Take a minute to look at the stories of resurrection in the last section. There are some main characters many of us can identify with. Let's take a minute to see which character represents where you are right now and see what action you can take to practice Life in the Spirit. Circle the character below who you most identify with. Then take the action suggested (or something else God speaks to you).

MARY & MARTHA
"I'm mourning lost or broken circumstances."
DO: Remind yourself that Jesus is mourning with you. Your loss breaks His heart. Consider writing a letter to what you feel you have lost. Share what you miss, what you are feeling, your regrets. Then, put the letter somewhere special to you. Mary and Martha buried their brother. He was part of who they were, and the loss they experienced brought them to a new understanding of who Jesus was — from Friend and Teacher, to Resurrection and Life.

EZEKIEL
"God is asking me to call the wind."
DO: Think about one person you can share the opportunity of new life with. Share it. Don't keep to yourself a gift so great. Don't know where to start? Maybe start by sharing your own story of rebirth and how you are learning to breathe.

LAZARUS
"I need to experience resurrection."
DO: Answer the voice of Jesus who is calling you out of the grave. Pray in this moment that the Holy Spirit would revive you. Pray that God would fill every part of you, even the parts that don't yet look like Jesus. Ask that the old would be gone as the new comes (2 Corinthians 5:17). This is our great solidarity with Christ, that because death was defeated by the power of His Spirit, death no longer has a hold on us. You have been made new.

If this is the first time you are praying to receive Jesus, tell someone you know who can walk with you on your new journey of Life.

If this is a resurrection of a different kind, celebrate with everyone you can the truth which marks every believer: I was broken, and now I am healed. I was lost and now I am found. I was dead and now I am alive.

I'm breathing now.

Every time we feel a need to breathe, it is a reminder that we have a God who gives us Life. It is a gift from God to draw us to himself.

We can't always fix what's wrong, but we can learn to breathe through it.

THROUGH IT is a promise that there is a way to the other side. The chasm of 'what ifs' and 'can't we justs' and 'it's not fairs' is not the end of the story.

I don't know what you are facing today. You might be in a bridgeless place, hopeful there can be a way. Or maybe you are staring at the ruins of what used to be a familiar path – the decay poignant from where you stand. The desperate feeling of being trapped or lost almost inescapable.

Let me remind you – we believe in a God who bridges gaps. Who fills the holes in our spirits with himself. Who, as Abraham believed, is the God who gives Life to the dead and calls into being things that were not. *Romans 4:17 (NIV)*

Our God is the one who called Lazarus out of the tomb after 4 days. He called death sleep and proved that nothing is too dead for Him to raise.

Is it possible we are looking in the wrong place for our bridge? That we believe the bridge will be from where we stand to the other side of our problem? On our level – in our perspective?

We stare into our not enough-ness, our unmet expectations, our all too real tragedies and wonder what the way across is.

What if instead of staring into our own lacking, we let the Holy Spirit lift our eyes to the fulfillment of Love, the cross of Christ – the great Bridge Builder.

With the cross, Jesus filled every divide between what is and what should be. As the cross was lifted, our eyes are lifted to see that the way across is really above. As we allow God to lift our eyes, to lift our spirits, we are taken up with the wind to the places only God can lead us. The higher we allow the Spirit to lift us, the smaller our problems appear. It's like looking at a city from an airplane – even the tallest skyscraper is hard to see from our higher perspective.

And, this is not about escape – this is about redemption. That from the perspective of the cross, we see things as they truly are. Finite. Momentary. Finished.

As we walk the way of the cross, across the chasm of our sin and shame and loss, we will find that the most important thing about following Jesus through our problems is just that – following Jesus.

We are so convinced that we are stuck because we see the destination we want across the chasm.

Truly following means you might not know the destination. Truly following means we will face pain and uncertainty.

What if we have extended all the effort in us to get from where we are, through our problem, to the other side, only to realize God was leading us to a completely different destination.

Let Jesus lead you. Let the Spirit lift you. Let our Great Life-Giver fill you.

Our bridges fail. Our plans fall short. Our breath runs out. From the beginning, we have failed to sustain our own lives.

And God never asked us to.

He wants to fill you. It was the first thing He did when He created us, He breathed the Breath of Life into the man's nostrils, and the man became a living person.

God wants you to be alive – fully alive.

Are you ready? Do you see it now?

You can learn to breathe.

You are learning to breathe.

Slow, deep, breaths.

Slow.

Deep breaths.

I cannot wait to see what life you will discover and share on this side of breathing.

TIME TO BREATHE

BREATHING PLAN

What you'll need:
- Your training schedule
- Your place
- Your control list
- Your truth cards
- Your Bible or Bible App
- Your journal and pen (or Sharpie!)
- Some courage
- Lots of commitment

What you'll do:
Make your own breathing plan. Set a regular time to go to your place to meet with God. Make a practice of the things we have explored in this book. Make yourself a rotation. Find a devotional you love. Have conversations and take action on the things you hear and write. This is YOUR BREATHING PLAN, so it needs to be full of the things which fill you up and spur you forward. Everyone is different, but we all need to be intentional about living a life breathing in the Spirit.

EXAMPLE (this is only a suggestion to get you started – you will have to find what is right for you)

SUNDAYS: Read one chapter in your Bible app.

Journal about the application you see and what the scripture means to you. Spend some time praying out loud about what you are learning.

MONDAYS: This is a good day for your control list. Remind yourself that you gave all the things you cannot control to Jesus. Maybe even pray that release out loud again. Then, pick the very first thing you CAN control and start one action toward making a change. Each Monday choose another action to take, and soon, you'll see your progress.

TUESDAYS: Write more truth cards. Explore a new topic every Tuesday. This week, look up verses on trust – next week, humility. Focus on 5 new scriptures every week for your 5 deep breaths. You might want to pick one to memorize. You'll notice as you start to memorize scripture that the breaths start to come easier.

WEDNESDAY: Start a reading plan in the Bible app. It can be topical or devotional. Spend some time reading what someone else has written about God (someone you trust) and see what you learn from them.

THURSDAY: Go through your list of accessory muscles. Write down something you can pray with them for, then tell them you are praying. Feel free to be specific when you share your prayers. It will grow your relationship deeper to share how the Holy Spirit is leading you to pray for one another. Don't be surprised when you start to get texts back with their prayers for you.

FRIDAY: Conversation day. Maybe you have a forgiveness conversation you need to have. Do you need to confess to God or someone you love (probably both)? Maybe you just need some encouragement? Set up a coffee date with the person you are feeling led to meet with. Pray about your conversation in your place. Write down your fears and hopes. After your conversation, journal about how it went and what you learned.

SATURDAY: Read one chapter in your Bible app. Journal about the application you see and what the scripture means to you. Share it with one person. It can be a family member, an accessory muscle or maybe someone who doesn't yet know Jesus. Sharing what we are authentically receiving is an incredible way to spread hope and peace to those we love. It's how we learn to breathe together.

One last thought . . .

Friend,

I don't know where you are in your journey of breathing and receiving, but I do know that God can do immeasurably more for us and in us than we could ask or think or imagine on our most creative day (Ephesians 3:20 – Jenni paraphrase).

This book is meant to be a diving board – a launching point into the deep Life to which you have been called. It is the first step, the wary jump, the trust fall into the deep waters in which the Spirit of God lives.

This is a call to deal with your problems, process your emotions, and to let the victory of Jesus lift your eyes above your circumstance and into all the richness Life in the Spirit has to offer. There is too much Life waiting for you to remain burdened and breathless.

May this spot mark a beginning. May the words on these pages whet your appetite for the truth of Scripture. Friend, I pray your hunger for the things of God will be insatiable.

Read more books. Study more Scripture. Meet with mentors. Mentor someone. Get involved in the life of the church. Serve your community. Love your family well. Discuss what Life in the Spirit looks like with those you are following Jesus with. Run hard. Rest well.

Breathe in. Breathe out.

Deep breaths.

There is always more of God.

deep breathing exercise.

Here is a simple deep breathing exercise* to help you relax. Please go see a counselor or a doctor if you are struggling with anxiety, emotions that feel too big for your body, or if you feel like you need more physical tools to deal with your circumstances.

1. Sit down comfortably, or lay down on a yoga mat, depending on your personal preference.
2. Place one of your hands on your stomach, just below your ribcage. Place the second hand over your chest.
3. Breathe in deeply through your nostrils, letting your first hand be pushed out by your stomach. You

should find that your chest stays stationary. Picture the air entering your toes and slowly rising up through your body – up through your hips, to your lungs, up to your face, and finally to the tips of your hair.

4. Start with counting to 4 on your inhale and counting to 5 on your exhale. *(The key is the exhale being slightly longer than the inhale)*

5. Breathe out through your lips, pursing them as if you were about to whistle. Gently guide the hand on your stomach inwards, helping to press out the breath. Picture the air leaving your body the way it came in.

6. Slowly repeat between 3 and 10 times. Each time, increase the length of your inhale and exhale as you feel comfortable.

There are many techniques and styles of deep breathing. Do what works for you. Look up some ideas, ask a counselor, read some more books.

Our physical health is so closely tied to our spiritual health. How do you cope with pain as it comes? Invest in learning the answer to that question and growing in those areas.

(this basic technique was taken from The Adrenal Fatigue Solution, and altered by me.)

resources.

I listed a few books and websites throughout the book I thought I'd recap for you here (plus a couple bonus resources):

- **Spotify Playlist:** Here is a list of songs I listened to on repeat while writing this book: byjenwaldron.com/playlist.

- **The Bible App** is an awesome tool. You can download it at Bible.com or in your device's app store. The Bible App has almost every translation as well as reading plans and devotionals. You can add friends and read scripture together.

- ***Nothing to Prove:*** *Why We Can Stop Trying So Hard* by Jennie Allen is a great book if you could use some encouragement.

- ***Unglued*** by Lysa TerKuerst is an excellent book on dealing with emotions.

- ***Soul Cravings*** by Erwin Raphael McManus is an amazing journey into feed your soul.

- ***The Book of Acts*** is a great place to read in the Bible to see the impact of a Spirit-filled life in a community of people. Same Spirit. Same church.

- **Shereadstruth.com + Hereadstruth.com** are both great daily devotional websites. They post a new devotional every day and have great resources you can purchase.

Breath in.

Breathe out.

Slowly.

There is always more.

Made in the USA
Lexington, KY
23 September 2017